MznLnx

Missing Links Exam Preps

Exam Prep for

Marketing Strategy: A Decision Focused Approach

Walker & Mullins, 6th Edition

The MznLnx Exam Prep is your link from the texbook and lecture to your exams.
The MznLnx Exam Preps are unauthorized and comprehensive reviews of your textbooks.

All material provided by MznLnx and Rico Publications (c) 2010
Textbook publishers and textbook authors do not particpate in or contribute to these reviews.

MznLnx

Rico Publications

Exam Prep for Marketing Strategy: A Decision Focused Approach
6th Edition
Walker & Mullins

Publisher: Raymond Houge
Assistant Editor: Michael Rouger
Text and Cover Designer: Lisa Buckner
Marketing Manager: Sara Swagger
Project Manager, Editorial Production: Jerry Emerson
Art Director: Vernon Lowerui

Product Manager: Dave Mason
Editorial Assitant: Rachel Guzmanji
Pedagogy: Debra Long
Cover Image: Jim Reed/Getty Images
Text and Cover Printer: City Printing, Inc.
Compositor: Media Mix, Inc.

(c) 2010 Rico Publications
ALL RIGHTS RESERVED. No part of this work covered by the copyright may be reproduced or used in any form or by an means--graphic, electronic, or mechanical, including photocopying, recording, taping, Web distribution, information storage, and retrieval systems, or in any other manner--without the written permission of the publisher.

Printed in the United States
ISBN:

For more information about our products, contact us at:
Dave.Mason@RicoPublications.com

For permission to use material from this text or product, submit a request online to:
Dave.Mason@RicoPublications.com

Contents

CHAPTER 1
Marketing-Oriented Perspectives Underlie Successful Strategies — 1

CHAPTER 2
Corporate Strategy Decisions and Their Marketing Implications — 8

CHAPTER 3
Business Strategies and Their Marketing Implications — 16

CHAPTER 4
Understanding Market Opportunities — 21

CHAPTER 5
Measuring Market Opportunities: Forecasting and Market Knowledge — 27

CHAPTER 6
Targeting Attractive Market Segments — 35

CHAPTER 7
Differentiation and Positioning — 38

CHAPTER 8
Marketing Strategies for New Market Entries — 42

CHAPTER 9
Strategies for Growth Markets — 51

CHAPTER 10
Strategies for Mature and Declining Markets — 52

CHAPTER 11
Marketing Strategies for the New Economy — 57

CHAPTER 12
Organizing and Planning for Effective Implementation — 68

CHAPTER 13
Measuring and Delivering Marketing Performance — 73

ANSWER KEY — 80

TO THE STUDENT

COMPREHENSIVE

The *MznLnx* Exam Prep series is designed to help you pass your exams. Editors at MznLnx review your textbooks and then prepare these practice exams to help you master the textbook material. Unlike study guides, workbooks, and practice tests provided by the texbook publisher and textbook authors, *MznLnx* gives you **all** of the material in each chapter in exam form, not just samples, so you can be sure to nail your exam.

MECHANICAL

The MznLnx Exam Prep series creates exams that will help you learn the subject matter as well as test you on your understanding. Each question is designed to help you master the concept. Just working through the exams, you gain an understanding of the subject--its a simple mechanical process that produces success.

INTEGRATED STUDY GUIDE AND REVIEW

MznLnx is not just a set of exams designed to test you, its also a comprehensive review of the subject content. Each exam question is also a review of the concept, making sure that you will get the answer correct without having to go to other sources of material. You learn as you go! Its the easiest way to pass an exam.

HUMOR

Studying can be tedious and dry. MznLnx's instructional design includes moderate humor within the exam questions on occassion, to break the tedium and revitalize the brain

Chapter 1. Marketing-Oriented Perspectives Underlie Successful Strategies

1. The acronym _____, is a psychographic segmentation. It was developed in the 1970s to explain changing U.S. values and lifestyles. It has since been reworked to enhance its ability to predict consumer behavior.

According to the _____ Framework, groups of people are arranged in a rectangle and are based on two dimensions. The vertical dimension segments people based on the degree to which they are innovative and have resources such as income, education, self-confidence, intelligence, leadership skills, and energy.

   a. VALS
   b. 180SearchAssistant
   c. 6-3-5 Brainwriting
   d. Power III

2. _____ is an advertisement in which a particular product specifically mentions a competitor by name for the express purpose of showing why the competitor is inferior to the product naming it.

This should not be confused with parody advertisements, where a fictional product is being advertised for the purpose of poking fun at the particular advertisement, nor should it be confused with the use of a coined brand name for the purpose of comparing the product without actually naming an actual competitor. ('Wikipedia tastes better and is less filling than the Encyclopedia Galactica.')

In the 1980s, during what has been referred to as the cola wars, soft-drink manufacturer Pepsi ran a series of advertisements where people, caught on hidden camera, in a blind taste test, chose Pepsi over rival Coca-Cola.

   a. Comparative advertising
   b. Cost per conversion
   c. Heavy-up
   d. GL-70

3. _____ refers to the overarching strategy of the diversified firm. Such a _____ answers the questions of 'in which businesses should we be in?' and 'how does being in these business create synergy and/or add to the competitive advantage of the corporation as a whole?'

Business strategy refers to the aggregated strategies of single business firm or a strategic business unit (SBU) in a diversified corporation. According to Michael Porter, a firm must formulate a business strategy that incorporates either cost leadership, differentiation or focus in order to achieve a sustainable competitive advantage and long-term success in its chosen arenas or industries.

a. Business strategy
b. Corporate strategy
c. Strategic business unit
d. Strategic group

4. _____ is defined by the American _____ Association as the activity, set of institutions, and processes for creating, communicating, delivering, and exchanging offerings that have value for customers, clients, partners, and society at large. The term developed from the original meaning which referred literally to going to market, as in shopping, or going to a market to sell goods or services.

_____ practice tends to be seen as a creative industry, which includes advertising, distribution and selling.

a. Customer acquisition management
b. Product naming
c. Marketing
d. Marketing myopia

5. Consumer market research is a form of applied sociology that concentrates on understanding the behaviours, whims and preferences, of consumers in a market-based economy, and aims to understand the effects and comparative success of marketing campaigns. The field of consumer _____ as a statistical science was pioneered by Arthur Nielsen with the founding of the ACNielsen Company In 1923.

Thus _____ is the systematic and objective identification, collection, analysis, and dissemination of information for the purpose of assisting management in decision making related to the identification and solution of problems and opportunities in marketing.

a. Marketing research process
b. Focus group
c. Marketing Research
d. Logit analysis

6. Founded in 1957, the _____ is one of the largest trade associations of market research and polling professionals. _____ has more than 3,000 members worldwide, representing all segments of the research industry. _____ advances, protects and promotes knowledge, standards, excellence, ethics, professional development and innovation for the global market and opinion research profession.

a. Power III
b. 180SearchAssistant
c. PRSA
d. Marketing Research Association

7. A _____ is a process that can allow an organization to concentrate its limited resources on the greatest opportunities to increase sales and achieve a sustainable competitive advantage. A _____ should be centered around the key concept that customer satisfaction is the main goal.

A _____ is most effective when it is an integral component of corporate strategy, defining how the organization will successfully engage customers, prospects, and competitors in the market arena.

a. Societal marketing
b. Marketing strategy
c. Psychographic
d. Cyberdoc

8. _____ is a measure of the strength of a brand, product, service relative to competitive offerings. There is often a geographic element to the competitive landscape. In defining _____, you must see to what extent a product, brand, or firm controls a product category in a given geographic area.

a. Discretionary spending
b. Market system
c. Productivity
d. Market dominance

9. A _____ is a plan of action designed to achieve a particular goal.

_____ is different from tactics. In military terms, tactics is concerned with the conduct of an engagement while _____ is concerned with how different engagements are linked.

a. Power III
b. 180SearchAssistant
c. Strategy
d. 6-3-5 Brainwriting

10. Competitiveness is a comparative concept of the ability and performance of a firm, sub-sector or country to sell and supply goods and/or services in a given market. Although widely used in economics and business management, the usefulness of the concept, particularly in the context of national competitiveness, is vigorously disputed by economists, such as Paul Krugman .

The term may also be applied to markets, where it is used to refer to the extent to which the market structure may be regarded as perfectly _____.

 a. Geographical pricing
 b. Customs union
 c. Free trade zone
 d. Competitive

11. _____ is, in very basic words, a position a firm occupies against its competitors.

According to Michael Porter, the three methods for creating a sustainable _____ are through:

1. Cost leadership - Cost advantage occurs when a firm delivers the same services as its competitors but at a lower cost;

2.

 a. 6-3-5 Brainwriting
 b. 180SearchAssistant
 c. Competitive advantage
 d. Power III

12. _____ is the term used to describe a situation where different entities cooperate advantageously for a final outcome. Simply defined, it means that the whole is greater than the sum of its parts. The essence of _____ is to value differences.
 a. Power III
 b. 6-3-5 Brainwriting
 c. Synergy
 d. 180SearchAssistant

13. A _____ is a collection of symbols, experiences and associations connected with a product, a service, a person or any other artifact or entity.

_____s have become increasingly important components of culture and the economy, now being described as 'cultural accessories and personal philosophies'.

Some people distinguish the psychological aspect of a _____ from the experiential aspect.

a. Brandable software
b. Store brand
c. Brand
d. Brand equity

14. In marketing, a _____ is the 'persona' of a corporation which is designed to accord with and facilitate the attainment of business objectives. It is usually visibly manifested by way of branding and the use of trademarks.

_____ comes into being when there is a common ownership of an organisational philosophy that is manifest in a distinct corporate culture -- the corporate personality.

a. Brand ambassador
b. Corporate identity
c. Brand recognition
d. Brand orientation

15. _____ in its literal sense is the process of transformation of local or regional phenomena into global ones. It can be described as a process by which the people of the world are unified into a single society and function together.

This process is a combination of economic, technological, sociocultural and political forces.

a. Power III
b. 180SearchAssistant
c. 6-3-5 Brainwriting
d. Globalization

16. Electronic commerce, commonly known as _____ or eCommerce, consists of the buying and selling of products or services over electronic systems such as the Internet and other computer networks. The amount of trade conducted electronically has grown extraordinarily with wide-spread Internet usage. A wide variety of commerce is conducted in this way, spurring and drawing on innovations in electronic funds transfer, supply chain management, Internet marketing, online transaction processing, electronic data interchange (EDI), inventory management systems, and automated data collection systems.

a. ADTECH
b. AMAX
c. ACNielsen
d. E-Commerce

17. Procter is a surname, and may also refer to:

- Bryan Waller Procter (pseud. Barry Cornwall), English poet
- Goodwin Procter, American law firm
- _____, consumer products multinational

a. Convergent
b. Flyer
c. Black PRies
d. Procter ' Gamble

18. A _____ is a subgroup of people or organizations sharing one or more characteristics that cause them to have similar product and/or service needs. A true _____ meets all of the following criteria: it is distinct from other segments (different segments have different needs), it is homogeneous within the segment (exhibits common needs); it responds similarly to a market stimulus, and it can be reached by a market intervention. The term is also used when consumers with identical product and/or service needs are divided up into groups so they can be charged different amounts.

a. Commercial planning
b. Production orientation
c. Customer insight
d. Market segment

19. In marketing, _____ has come to mean the process by which marketers try to create an image or identity in the minds of their target market for its product, brand, or organization. It is the 'relative competitive comparison' their product occupies in a given market as perceived by the target market.

Re-_____ involves changing the identity of a product, relative to the identity of competing products, in the collective minds of the target market.

a. Containerization
b. Moratorium
c. Positioning
d. GE matrix

20. A _____ is a written document that details the necessary actions to achieve one or more marketing objectives. It can be for a product or service, a brand, or a product line. _____s cover between one and five years.

a. Marketing strategy
b. Disruptive technology
c. Prosumer
d. Marketing plan

Chapter 2. Corporate Strategy Decisions and Their Marketing Implications

1. Competitiveness is a comparative concept of the ability and performance of a firm, sub-sector or country to sell and supply goods and/or services in a given market. Although widely used in economics and business management, the usefulness of the concept, particularly in the context of national competitiveness, is vigorously disputed by economists, such as Paul Krugman .

The term may also be applied to markets, where it is used to refer to the extent to which the market structure may be regarded as perfectly _____.

   a. Geographical pricing
   b. Customs union
   c. Free trade zone
   d. Competitive

2. _____ is, in very basic words, a position a firm occupies against its competitors.

According to Michael Porter, the three methods for creating a sustainable _____ are through:

1. Cost leadership - Cost advantage occurs when a firm delivers the same services as its competitors but at a lower cost;

2.

   a. Competitive advantage
   b. Power III
   c. 6-3-5 Brainwriting
   d. 180SearchAssistant

3. _____ refers to the overarching strategy of the diversified firm. Such a _____ answers the questions of 'in which businesses should we be in?' and 'how does being in these business create synergy and/or add to the competitive advantage of the corporation as a whole?'

Business strategy refers to the aggregated strategies of single business firm or a strategic business unit (SBU) in a diversified corporation. According to Michael Porter, a firm must formulate a business strategy that incorporates either cost leadership, differentiation or focus in order to achieve a sustainable competitive advantage and long-term success in its chosen arenas or industries.

   a. Corporate strategy
   b. Strategic group
   c. Strategic business unit
   d. Business strategy

Chapter 2. Corporate Strategy Decisions and Their Marketing Implications

4. _____ is the term used to describe a situation where different entities cooperate advantageously for a final outcome. Simply defined, it means that the whole is greater than the sum of its parts. The essence of _____ is to value differences.
   a. Synergy
   b. 6-3-5 Brainwriting
   c. Power III
   d. 180SearchAssistant

5. A _____ is a collection of symbols, experiences and associations connected with a product, a service, a person or any other artifact or entity.

   _____s have become increasingly important components of culture and the economy, now being described as 'cultural accessories and personal philosophies'.

   Some people distinguish the psychological aspect of a _____ from the experiential aspect.

   a. Brand equity
   b. Brand
   c. Store brand
   d. Brandable software

6. In marketing, a _____ is the 'persona' of a corporation which is designed to accord with and facilitate the attainment of business objectives. It is usually visibly manifested by way of branding and the use of trademarks.

   _____ comes into being when there is a common ownership of an organisational philosophy that is manifest in a distinct corporate culture -- the corporate personality.

   a. Brand recognition
   b. Brand ambassador
   c. Brand orientation
   d. Corporate identity

7. A _____ is a plan of action designed to achieve a particular goal.

   _____ is different from tactics. In military terms, tactics is concerned with the conduct of an engagement while _____ is concerned with how different engagements are linked.

Chapter 2. Corporate Strategy Decisions and Their Marketing Implications

   a. Power III
   b. 180SearchAssistant
   c. 6-3-5 Brainwriting
   d. Strategy

8. _____ is a branch of philosophy which seeks to address questions about morality, such as how a moral outcome can be achieved in a specific situation (applied _____), how moral values should be determined (normative _____), what moral values people actually abide by (descriptive _____), what the fundamental semantic, ontological, and epistemic nature of _____ or morality is (meta-_____), and how moral capacity or moral agency develops and what its nature is (moral psychology.)

Socrates was one of the first Greek philosophers to encourage both scholars and the common citizen to turn their attention from the outside world to the condition of man. In this view, Knowledge having a bearing on human life was placed highest, all other knowledge being secondary.

   a. ADTECH
   b. ACNielsen
   c. AMAX
   d. Ethics

9. A _____ is a set of consistent ethic values (more specifically the personal and cultural values) and measures used for the purpose of ethical or ideological integrity. A well defined _____ is a moral code.

One or more people can hold a _____.

   a. Power III
   b. 180SearchAssistant
   c. 6-3-5 Brainwriting
   d. Value system

10. A personal and cultural _____ is a relative ethic _____, an assumption upon which implementation can be extrapolated. A _____ system is a set of consistent _____s and measures that is soo not true. A principle _____ is a foundation upon which other _____s and measures of integrity are based.
   a. Perceptual maps
   b. Value
   c. Supreme Court of the United States
   d. Package-on-Package

Chapter 2. Corporate Strategy Decisions and Their Marketing Implications

11. A mutual _____ or stockholder is an individual or company (including a corporation) that legally owns one or more shares of stock in a joint stock company. A company's _____s collectively own that company. Thus, the typical goal of such companies is to enhance _____ value.
    a. Power III
    b. Shareholder
    c. Total shareholder return
    d. 180SearchAssistant

12. _____ is a business buzz term, which implies that the ultimate measure of a company's success is to enrich shareholders. It became popular during the 1980s, and is particularly associated with former CEO of General Electric, Jack Welch. In March 2009, Welch openly turned his back on the concept, calling shardeholder value 'the dumbest idea in the world'.
    a. 6-3-5 Brainwriting
    b. Power III
    c. 180SearchAssistant
    d. Shareholder value

13. _____s is the social science that studies the production, distribution, and consumption of goods and services. The term _____s comes from the Ancient Greek οἰκονομία from οἶκος (oikos, 'house') + νόμος (nomos, 'custom' or 'law'), hence 'rules of the house(hold)'. Current _____ models developed out of the broader field of political economy in the late 19th century, owing to a desire to use an empirical approach more akin to the physical sciences.
    a. ACNielsen
    b. ADTECH
    c. Economic
    d. Industrial organization

14. The _____ of a good or service has puzzled economists since the beginning of the discipline. First, economists tried to estimate the value of a good to an individual alone, and extend that definition to goods which can be exchanged. From this analysis came the concepts value in use and value in exchange.
    a. AMAX
    b. ACNielsen
    c. ADTECH
    d. Economic value

15. _____ is the price at which an asset would trade in a competitive Walrasian auction setting. _____ is often used interchangeably with open _____, fair value or fair _____, although these terms have distinct definitions in different standards, and may differ in some circumstances.

International Valuation Standards defines _____ as 'the estimated amount for which a property should exchange on the date of valuation between a willing buyer and a willing seller in an arm's-length transaction after proper marketing wherein the parties had each acted knowledgeably, prudently, and without compulsion.'

_____ is a concept distinct from market price, which is 'the price at which one can transact', while _____ is 'the true underlying value' according to theoretical standards.

- a. 180SearchAssistant
- b. Power III
- c. Restructuring
- d. Market value

16. _____ is defined by the American _____ Association as the activity, set of institutions, and processes for creating, communicating, delivering, and exchanging offerings that have value for customers, clients, partners, and society at large. The term developed from the original meaning which referred literally to going to market, as in shopping, or going to a market to sell goods or services.

_____ practice tends to be seen as a creative industry, which includes advertising, distribution and selling.

- a. Customer acquisition management
- b. Marketing myopia
- c. Product naming
- d. Marketing

17. _____ refers to the additional value of a commodity over the cost of commodities used to produce it from the previous stage of production. An example is the price of gasoline at the pump over the price of the oil in it. In national accounts used in macroeconomics, it refers to the contribution of the factors of production, i.e., land, labor, and capital goods, to raising the value of a product and corresponds to the incomes received by the owners of these factors. The factors of production provide 'services' which raise the unit price of a product (X) relative to the cost per unit of intermediate goods used up in the production of X. _____ is shared between the factors of production (capital, labor, also human capital), giving rise to issues of distribution.
- a. Value added
- b. Consumer spending
- c. Deregulation
- d. Power III

18. In microeconomics and management, the term _____ describes a style of management control. Vertically integrated companies are united through a hierarchy with a common owner. Usually each member of the hierarchy produces a different product or (market-specific) service, and the products combine to satisfy a common need.

Chapter 2. Corporate Strategy Decisions and Their Marketing Implications

a. Flanking marketing warfare strategies
b. Power III
c. Mass customization
d. Vertical integration

19. The _____ is a chart that had been created by Bruce Henderson for the Boston Consulting Group in 1970 to help corporations with analyzing their business units or product lines. This helps the company allocate resources and is used as an analytical tool in brand marketing, product management, strategic management, and portfolio analysis.

a. AStore
b. Sampling
c. Sports Marketing Group
d. BCG matrix

20. A _____ is a set of companies with interlocking business relationships and shareholdings. It is a type of business group.

The prototypical _____ are those which appeared in Japan during the 'economic miracle' following World War II.

a. 180SearchAssistant
b. Power III
c. 6-3-5 Brainwriting
d. Keiretsu

21. _____, or Value optimized pricing is a business strategy. It sets selling prices on the perceived value to the customer, rather than on the actual cost of the product, the market price, competitors prices, or the historical price.

The goal of _____ is to align price with value delivered.

a. Money back guarantee
b. Service-profit chain
c. Jobbing house
d. Value-based pricing

22. _____, in strategic management and marketing, is the percentage or proportion of the total available market or market segment that is being serviced by a company. It can be expressed as a company's sales revenue (from that market) divided by the total sales revenue available in that market. It can also be expressed as a company's unit sales volume (in a market) divided by the total volume of units sold in that market.

Chapter 2. Corporate Strategy Decisions and Their Marketing Implications

   a. Customer relationship management
   b. Market share
   c. Cyberdoc
   d. Demand generation

23. _____ in organizations and public policy is both the organizational process of creating and maintaining a plan; and the psychological process of thinking about the activities required to create a desired goal on some scale. As such, it is a fundamental property of intelligent behavior. This thought process is essential to the creation and refinement of a plan, or integration of it with other plans, that is, it combines forecasting of developments with the preparation of scenarios of how to react to them.
   a. Planning
   b. Power III
   c. 6-3-5 Brainwriting
   d. 180SearchAssistant

24. Human beings are also considered to be _____ because they have the ability to change raw materials into valuable _____. The term Human _____ can also be defined as the skills, energies, talents, abilities and knowledge that are used for the production of goods or the rendering of services. While taking into account human beings as _____, the following things have to be kept in mind:

   - The size of the population
   - The capabilities of the individuals in that population

Many _____ cannot be consumed in their original form. They have to be processed in order to change them into more usable commodities.

   a. Power III
   b. 180SearchAssistant
   c. 6-3-5 Brainwriting
   d. Resources

25. In business, a _____ is a product or a business unit that generates unusually high profit margins: so high that it is responsible for a large amount of a company's operating profit. This profit far exceeds the amount necessary to maintain the _____ business, and the excess is used by the business for other purposes.

A firm is said to be acting as a _____ when its earnings per share (EPS) is equal to its dividends per share (DPS), or in other words, when a firm pays out 100% of its free cash flow (FCF) to its shareholders as dividends at the end of each accounting term.

a. Goal setting
b. Corporate transparency
c. Crisis management
d. Cash cow

Chapter 3. Business Strategies and Their Marketing Implications

1. _____ is the term used to describe a situation where different entities cooperate advantageously for a final outcome. Simply defined, it means that the whole is greater than the sum of its parts. The essence of _____ is to value differences.
   a. 6-3-5 Brainwriting
   b. Power III
   c. 180SearchAssistant
   d. Synergy

2. A _____ is a collection of symbols, experiences and associations connected with a product, a service, a person or any other artifact or entity.

   _____s have become increasingly important components of culture and the economy, now being described as 'cultural accessories and personal philosophies'.

   Some people distinguish the psychological aspect of a _____ from the experiential aspect.

   a. Store brand
   b. Brandable software
   c. Brand equity
   d. Brand

3. In marketing, a _____ is the 'persona' of a corporation which is designed to accord with and facilitate the attainment of business objectives. It is usually visibly manifested by way of branding and the use of trademarks.

   _____ comes into being when there is a common ownership of an organisational philosophy that is manifest in a distinct corporate culture -- the corporate personality.

   a. Brand orientation
   b. Brand recognition
   c. Corporate identity
   d. Brand ambassador

4. Human beings are also considered to be _____ because they have the ability to change raw materials into valuable _____. The term Human _____ can also be defined as the skills, energies, talents, abilities and knowledge that are used for the production of goods or the rendering of services. While taking into account human beings as _____, the following things have to be kept in mind:

   - The size of the population
   - The capabilities of the individuals in that population

Chapter 3. Business Strategies and Their Marketing Implications

Many _____ cannot be consumed in their original form. They have to be processed in order to change them into more usable commodities.

a. 6-3-5 Brainwriting
b. 180SearchAssistant
c. Power III
d. Resources

5. A _____ is a plan of action designed to achieve a particular goal.

_____ is different from tactics. In military terms, tactics is concerned with the conduct of an engagement while _____ is concerned with how different engagements are linked.

a. 180SearchAssistant
b. 6-3-5 Brainwriting
c. Power III
d. Strategy

6. _____ is understood as a business unit within the overall corporate identity which is distinguishable from other business because it serves a defined external market where management can conduct strategic planning in relation to products and markets. When companies become really large, they are best thought of as being composed of a number of businesses (or _____ s.)

In the broader domain of strategic management, the phrase '_____' came into use in the 1960s, largely as a result of General Electric's many units.

a. Cost leadership
b. Business strategy
c. Corporate strategy
d. Strategic business unit

7. Competitiveness is a comparative concept of the ability and performance of a firm, sub-sector or country to sell and supply goods and/or services in a given market. Although widely used in economics and business management, the usefulness of the concept, particularly in the context of national competitiveness, is vigorously disputed by economists, such as Paul Krugman .

The term may also be applied to markets, where it is used to refer to the extent to which the market structure may be regarded as perfectly _____.

a. Competitive
b. Free trade zone
c. Geographical pricing
d. Customs union

8. In economics, business, retail, and accounting, a _____ is the value of money that has been used up to produce something, and hence is not available for use anymore. In economics, a _____ is an alternative that is given up as a result of a decision. In business, the _____ may be one of acquisition, in which case the amount of money expended to acquire it is counted as _____.
   a. Transaction cost
   b. Variable cost
   c. Cost
   d. Fixed costs

9. _____ is a concept developed by Michael Porter, used in business strategy. It describes a way to establish the competitive advantage. _____, in basic words, means the lowest cost of operation in the industry.
   a. Chaotics
   b. Strategic group
   c. Cost leadership
   d. Corporate strategy

10. _____ is a measure of the strength of a brand, product, service relative to competitive offerings. There is often a geographic element to the competitive landscape. In defining _____, you must see to what extent a product, brand, or firm controls a product category in a given geographic area.
    a. Discretionary spending
    b. Market system
    c. Productivity
    d. Market dominance

11. _____ is an advertisement in which a particular product specifically mentions a competitor by name for the express purpose of showing why the competitor is inferior to the product naming it.

This should not be confused with parody advertisements, where a fictional product is being advertised for the purpose of poking fun at the particular advertisement, nor should it be confused with the use of a coined brand name for the purpose of comparing the product without actually naming an actual competitor. ('Wikipedia tastes better and is less filling than the Encyclopedia Galactica.')

Chapter 3. Business Strategies and Their Marketing Implications

In the 1980s, during what has been referred to as the cola wars, soft-drink manufacturer Pepsi ran a series of advertisements where people, caught on hidden camera, in a blind taste test, chose Pepsi over rival Coca-Cola.

a. GL-70
b. Cost per conversion
c. Heavy-up
d. Comparative advertising

12. In business, a _____ is a product or a business unit that generates unusually high profit margins: so high that it is responsible for a large amount of a company's operating profit. This profit far exceeds the amount necessary to maintain the _____ business, and the excess is used by the business for other purposes.

A firm is said to be acting as a _____ when its earnings per share (EPS) is equal to its dividends per share (DPS), or in other words, when a firm pays out 100% of its free cash flow (FCF) to its shareholders as dividends at the end of each accounting term.

a. Corporate transparency
b. Goal setting
c. Crisis management
d. Cash cow

13. _____ is defined by the American _____ Association as the activity, set of institutions, and processes for creating, communicating, delivering, and exchanging offerings that have value for customers, clients, partners, and society at large. The term developed from the original meaning which referred literally to going to market, as in shopping, or going to a market to sell goods or services.

_____ practice tends to be seen as a creative industry, which includes advertising, distribution and selling.

a. Product naming
b. Marketing myopia
c. Customer acquisition management
d. Marketing

14. _____ is one of the four elements of marketing mix. An organization or set of organizations (go-betweens) involved in the process of making a product or service available for use or consumption by a consumer or business user.

The other three parts of the marketing mix are product, pricing, and promotion.

Chapter 3. Business Strategies and Their Marketing Implications

a. Better Living Through Chemistry
b. Comparison-Shopping agent
c. Japan Advertising Photographers' Association
d. Distribution

15. _____ is one of the four Ps of the marketing mix. The other three aspects are product, promotion, and place. It is also a key variable in microeconomic price allocation theory.
   a. Pricing
   b. Competitor indexing
   c. Price
   d. Relationship based pricing

16. _____ involves disseminating information about a product, product line, brand, or company. It is one of the four key aspects of the marketing mix. (The other three elements are product marketing, pricing, and distribution). P>_____ is generally sub-divided into two parts:

   - Above the line _____: Promotion in the media (e.g. TV, radio, newspapers, Internet and Mobile Phones) in which the advertiser pays an advertising agency to place the ad
   - Below the line _____: All other _____. Much of this is intended to be subtle enough for the consumer to be unaware that _____ is taking place. E.g. sponsorship, product placement, endorsements, sales _____, merchandising, direct mail, personal selling, public relations, trade shows

   a. Cashmere Agency
   b. Bottling lines
   c. Promotion
   d. Davie Brown Index

17. In microeconomics and management, the term _____ describes a style of management control. Vertically integrated companies are united through a hierarchy with a common owner. Usually each member of the hierarchy produces a different product or (market-specific) service, and the products combine to satisfy a common need.
   a. Power III
   b. Flanking marketing warfare strategies
   c. Mass customization
   d. Vertical integration

Chapter 4. Understanding Market Opportunities

1. An _____ is the manufacturing of a good or service within a category. Although _____ is a broad term for any kind of economic production, in economics and urban planning _____ is a synonym for the secondary sector, which is a type of economic activity involved in the manufacturing of raw materials into goods and products.

There are four key industrial economic sectors: the primary sector, largely raw material extraction industries such as mining and farming; the secondary sector, involving refining, construction, and manufacturing; the tertiary sector, which deals with services (such as law and medicine) and distribution of manufactured goods; and the quaternary sector, a relatively new type of knowledge _____ focusing on technological research, design and development such as computer programming, and biochemistry.

   a. ADTECH
   b. Industry
   c. AMAX
   d. ACNielsen

2. _____ or _____ data refers to selected population characteristics as used in government, marketing or opinion research, or the _____ profiles used in such research. Note the distinction from the term 'demography' Commonly-used _____ include race, age, income, disabilities, mobility (in terms of travel time to work or number of vehicles available), educational attainment, home ownership, employment status, and even location.
   a. African Americans
   b. AStore
   c. Albert Einstein
   d. Demographic

3. _____ is the change in population over time, and can be quantified as the change in the number of individuals in a population using 'per unit time' for measurement. The term _____ can technically refer to any species, but almost always refers to humans, and it is often used informally for the more specific demographic term _____ rate , and is often used to refer specifically to the growth of the population of the world.

Simple models of _____ include the Malthusian Growth Model and the logistic model.

   a. 180SearchAssistant
   b. Power III
   c. 6-3-5 Brainwriting
   d. Population growth

Chapter 4. Understanding Market Opportunities

4. Procter is a surname, and may also refer to:

- Bryan Waller Procter (pseud. Barry Cornwall), English poet
- Goodwin Procter, American law firm
- _____, consumer products multinational

a. Flyer
b. Convergent
c. Black PRies
d. Procter ' Gamble

5. _____ is a form of applied ethics that examines ethical principles and moral or ethical problems that arise in a business environment. It applies to all aspects of business conduct and is relevant to the conduct of individuals and business organizations as a whole. Applied ethics is a field of ethics that deals with ethical questions in many fields such as medical, technical, legal and _____.
a. 180SearchAssistant
b. 6-3-5 Brainwriting
c. Power III
d. Business ethics

6. _____s is the social science that studies the production, distribution, and consumption of goods and services. The term _____s comes from the Ancient Greek oá¼°κονομῖα from oá¼¶κος (oikos, 'house') + vϓμος (nomos, 'custom' or 'law'), hence 'rules of the house(hold)'. Current _____ models developed out of the broader field of political economy in the late 19th century, owing to a desire to use an empirical approach more akin to the physical sciences.
a. Economic
b. ADTECH
c. Industrial organization
d. ACNielsen

7. _____ is a branch of philosophy which seeks to address questions about morality, such as how a moral outcome can be achieved in a specific situation (applied _____), how moral values should be determined (normative _____), what moral values people actually abide by (descriptive _____), what the fundamental semantic, ontological, and epistemic nature of _____ or morality is (meta-_____), and how moral capacity or moral agency develops and what its nature is (moral psychology.)

Socrates was one of the first Greek philosophers to encourage both scholars and the common citizen to turn their attention from the outside world to the condition of man. In this view, Knowledge having a bearing on human life was placed highest, all other knowledge being secondary.

Chapter 4. Understanding Market Opportunities

a. ADTECH
b. AMAX
c. ACNielsen
d. Ethics

8. _____ is a process by which government's control over businesses and individuals is reduced or eliminated. It is the removal of some governmental controls over a market. _____ does not mean elimination of laws against fraud, but eliminating or reducing government control of how business is done, thereby moving toward a more free market.
   a. Power III
   b. Consumer spending
   c. Value added
   d. Deregulation

9. _____ refers to 'controlling human or societal behaviour by rules or restrictions.' _____ can take many forms: legal restrictions promulgated by a government authority, self-_____, social _____, co-_____ and market _____. One can consider _____ as actions of conduct imposing sanctions (such as a fine.) This action of administrative law, or implementing regulatory law, may be contrasted with statutory or case law.
   a. Regulation
   b. Rule of four
   c. Non-conventional trademark
   d. CAN-SPAM

10. Regulation refers to 'controlling human or societal behaviour by rules or restrictions.' Regulation can take many forms: legal restrictions promulgated by a government authority, self-regulation, social regulation (e.g. norms), co-regulation and market regulation. One can consider regulation as actions of conduct imposing sanctions (such as a fine.) This action of administrative law, or implementing _____ law, may be contrasted with statutory or case law.
    a. Robinson-Patman Act
    b. Privacy law
    c. Regulatory
    d. Right to Financial Privacy Act

11. A _____ is a plan of action designed to achieve a particular goal.

    _____ is different from tactics. In military terms, tactics is concerned with the conduct of an engagement while _____ is concerned with how different engagements are linked.

Chapter 4. Understanding Market Opportunities

   a. Strategy
   b. Power III
   c. 6-3-5 Brainwriting
   d. 180SearchAssistant

12. Competitiveness is a comparative concept of the ability and performance of a firm, sub-sector or country to sell and supply goods and/or services in a given market. Although widely used in economics and business management, the usefulness of the concept, particularly in the context of national competitiveness, is vigorously disputed by economists, such as Paul Krugman .

The term may also be applied to markets, where it is used to refer to the extent to which the market structure may be regarded as perfectly _____.

   a. Geographical pricing
   b. Competitive
   c. Free trade zone
   d. Customs union

13. A supply chain is the system of organizations, people, technology, activities, information and resources involved in moving a product or service from _____ to customer. Supply chain activities transform natural resources, raw materials and components into a finished product that is delivered to the end customer. In sophisticated supply chain systems, used products may re-enter the supply chain at any point where residual value is recyclable.
   a. Product line extension
   b. Bringin' Home the Oil
   c. Rebate
   d. Supplier

14. A _____ is a documented investigation of a Market that is used to inform a firm's planning activities particularly around decision of: inventory, purchase, work force expansion/contraction, facility expansion, purchases of capital equipment, promotional activities, and many other aspects of a company.

Not all managers are asked to conduct a _____, but all managers must make decisions using _____ data and understand how the data was derived. So all managers need a reasonable understanding of the tools most used for making sales forecasts and analyzing markets.

a. Cross tabulation
b. Preference regression
c. Market analysis
d. Simple random sampling

15. _____ was originally coined by Austrian psychologist Alfred Adler in 1929. The current broader sense of the word dates from 1961.

In sociology, a _____ is the way a person lives.

a. Lifestyle
b. 180SearchAssistant
c. 6-3-5 Brainwriting
d. Power III

16. _____, in strategic management and marketing, is the percentage or proportion of the total available market or market segment that is being serviced by a company. It can be expressed as a company's sales revenue (from that market) divided by the total sales revenue available in that market. It can also be expressed as a company's unit sales volume (in a market) divided by the total volume of units sold in that market.
a. Demand generation
b. Cyberdoc
c. Market Share
d. Customer relationship management

17. _____ is defined by the American _____ Association as the activity, set of institutions, and processes for creating, communicating, delivering, and exchanging offerings that have value for customers, clients, partners, and society at large. The term developed from the original meaning which referred literally to going to market, as in shopping, or going to a market to sell goods or services.

_____ practice tends to be seen as a creative industry, which includes advertising, distribution and selling.

a. Customer acquisition management
b. Marketing
c. Product naming
d. Marketing myopia

18. _____ is a business discipline which is focused on the practical application of marketing techniques and the management of a firm's marketing resources and activities. Marketing managers are often responsible for influencing the level, timing, and composition of customer demand accepted definition of the term. In part, this is because the role of a marketing manager can vary significantly based on a business' size, corporate culture, and industry context.

   a. Door-to-door
   b. Business structure
   c. Performance-based advertising
   d. Marketing Management

19. The _____ is a publication of the United States Census Bureau, an agency of the United States Department of Commerce. Published annually since 1878, the statistics describe social and economic conditions in the United States.

In 1975 a two volume Historical Statistics of the United States, Colonial Times to 1970 Bicentennial Edition was published.

   a. Power III
   b. 180SearchAssistant
   c. 6-3-5 Brainwriting
   d. Statistical Abstract of the United States

Chapter 5. Measuring Market Opportunities: Forecasting and Market Knowledge

1. _____ is the process of estimation in unknown situations. Prediction is a similar, but more general term. Both can refer to estimation of time series, cross-sectional or longitudinal data.

   a. Forecasting
   b. 6-3-5 Brainwriting
   c. Power III
   d. 180SearchAssistant

2. _____ is defined by the American _____ Association as the activity, set of institutions, and processes for creating, communicating, delivering, and exchanging offerings that have value for customers, clients, partners, and society at large. The term developed from the original meaning which referred literally to going to market, as in shopping, or going to a market to sell goods or services.

   _____ practice tends to be seen as a creative industry, which includes advertising, distribution and selling.

   a. Product naming
   b. Customer acquisition management
   c. Marketing myopia
   d. Marketing

3. Consumer market research is a form of applied sociology that concentrates on understanding the behaviours, whims and preferences, of consumers in a market-based economy, and aims to understand the effects and comparative success of marketing campaigns. The field of consumer _____ as a statistical science was pioneered by Arthur Nielsen with the founding of the ACNielsen Company in 1923.

   Thus _____ is the systematic and objective identification, collection, analysis, and dissemination of information for the purpose of assisting management in decision making related to the identification and solution of problems and opportunities in marketing.

   a. Logit analysis
   b. Focus group
   c. Marketing research process
   d. Marketing research

4. _____ is either an activity of a living being (such as a human), consisting of receiving knowledge of the outside world through the senses, or the recording of data using scientific instruments. The term may also refer to any datum collected during this activity.

   The scientific method requires _____s of nature to formulate and test hypotheses.

a. ACNielsen
b. ADTECH
c. AMAX
d. Observation

5. A _____ attribute is one that exists in a range of magnitudes, and can therefore be measured. Measurements of any particular _____ property are expressed as a specific quantity, referred to as a unit, multiplied by a number. Examples of physical quantities are distance, mass, and time.

a. BeyondROI
b. Dolly Dimples
c. Lifestyle city
d. Quantitative

6. A _____ is a form of qualitative research in which a group of people are asked about their attitude towards a product, service, concept, advertisement, idea, or packaging. Questions are asked in an interactive group setting where participants are free to talk with other group members.

Ernest Dichter originated the idea of having a 'group therapy' for products and this process is what became known as a _____.

a. Cross tabulation
b. Focus group
c. Logit analysis
d. Marketing research process

7. A _____, in the field of business and marketing, is a geographic region or demographic group used to gauge the viability of a product or service in the mass market prior to a wide scale roll-out. The criteria used to judge the acceptability of a _____ region or group include:

1. a population that is demographically similar to the proposed target market; and
2. relative isolation from densely populated media markets so that advertising to the test audience can be efficient and economical.

The _____ ideally aims to duplicate 'everything' - promotion and distribution as well as `product' - on a smaller scale. The technique replicates, typically in one area, what is planned to occur in a national launch; and the results are very carefully monitored, so that they can be extrapolated to projected national results. The `area' may be any one of the following:

- Television area
- Test town
- Residential neighborhood
- Test site

A number of decisions have to be taken about any _____:

- Which _____?
- What is to be tested?
- How long a test?
- What are the success criteria?

The simple go or no-go decision, together with the related reduction of risk, is normally the main justification for the expense of _____s. At the same time, however, such _____s can be used to test specific elements of a new product's marketing mix; possibly the version of the product itself, the promotional message and media spend, the distribution channels and the price.

 a. Preadolescence
 b. Power III
 c. 180SearchAssistant
 d. Test market

8. A _____ is a collection of symbols, experiences and associations connected with a product, a service, a person or any other artifact or entity.

_____s have become increasingly important components of culture and the economy, now being described as 'cultural accessories and personal philosophies'.

Some people distinguish the psychological aspect of a _____ from the experiential aspect.

 a. Brand equity
 b. Brandable software
 c. Store brand
 d. Brand

Chapter 5. Measuring Market Opportunities: Forecasting and Market Knowledge

9. _____ is the process by which a new idea or new product is accepted by the market. The rate of _____ is the speed that the new idea spreads from one consumer to the next. Adoption is similar to _____ except that it deals with the psychological processes an individual goes through, rather than an aggregate market process.
   a. Market development
   b. Perceptual maps
   c. Kano model
   d. Diffusion

10. _____ is a theory of how, why, and at what rate new ideas and technology spread through cultures. Everett Rogers introduced it in his 1962 book, _____s, writing that 'Diffusion is the process by which an innovation is communicated through certain channels over time among the members of a social system.' The adoption curve becomes an s-curve when cumulative adoption is used.

Rogers theorized that innovations would spread through a community in an S curve, as the early adopters select the innovation (which may be a technology) first, followed by the majority, until a technology or innovation has reached its saturation point in a community.

According to Rogers, diffusion research centers on the conditions which increase or decrease the likelihood that a new idea, product, or practice will be adopted by members of a given culture.

   a. 6-3-5 Brainwriting
   b. 180SearchAssistant
   c. Power III
   d. Diffusion of innovation

11. _____ is a business discipline which is focused on the practical application of marketing techniques and the management of a firm's marketing resources and activities. Marketing managers are often responsible for influencing the level, timing, and composition of customer demand accepted definition of the term. In part, this is because the role of a marketing manager can vary significantly based on a business' size, corporate culture, and industry context.
   a. Business structure
   b. Performance-based advertising
   c. Door-to-door
   d. Marketing Management

12. _____ is one of the four elements of marketing mix. An organization or set of organizations (go-betweens) involved in the process of making a product or service available for use or consumption by a consumer or business user.

The other three parts of the marketing mix are product, pricing, and promotion.

Chapter 5. Measuring Market Opportunities: Forecasting and Market Knowledge

a. Comparison-Shopping agent
b. Better Living Through Chemistry
c. Japan Advertising Photographers' Association
d. Distribution

13. Competitiveness is a comparative concept of the ability and performance of a firm, sub-sector or country to sell and supply goods and/or services in a given market. Although widely used in economics and business management, the usefulness of the concept, particularly in the context of national competitiveness, is vigorously disputed by economists, such as Paul Krugman .

The term may also be applied to markets, where it is used to refer to the extent to which the market structure may be regarded as perfectly _____.

a. Customs union
b. Free trade zone
c. Competitive
d. Geographical pricing

14. _____ is, in very basic words, a position a firm occupies against its competitors.

According to Michael Porter, the three methods for creating a sustainable _____ are through:

1. Cost leadership - Cost advantage occurs when a firm delivers the same services as its competitors but at a lower cost;

2.

a. 6-3-5 Brainwriting
b. 180SearchAssistant
c. Power III
d. Competitive advantage

15. A _____ is a structured collection of records or data that is stored in a computer system. The structure is achieved by organizing the data according to a _____ model. The model in most common use today is the relational model.
a. 180SearchAssistant
b. Power III
c. Database
d. 6-3-5 Brainwriting

Chapter 5. Measuring Market Opportunities: Forecasting and Market Knowledge

16. The _____ is a professional association for marketers. As of 2008 it had approximately 40,000 members. There are collegiate chapters on 250 campuses.
    a. American Marketing Association
    b. ACNielsen
    c. ADTECH
    d. AMAX

17. _____ is a form of direct marketing using databases of customers or potential customers to generate personalized communications in order to promote a product or service for marketing purposes. The method of communication can be any addressable medium, as in direct marketing.

The distinction between direct and _____ stems primarily from the attention paid to the analysis of data.

   a. Direct marketing
   b. Database marketing
   c. Power III
   d. Direct Marketing Associations

18. _____, also referred to as i-marketing, web marketing, online marketing is the marketing of products or services over the Internet.

The Internet has brought many unique benefits to marketing, one of which being lower costs for the distribution of information and media to a global audience. The interactive nature of _____, both in terms of providing instant response and eliciting responses, is a unique quality of the medium.

   a. Internet marketing
   b. AMAX
   c. ACNielsen
   d. ADTECH

19. _____ often refers to either primary or secondary research. Secondary research involves a company using information compiled from various sources, which is about a new or existing product. The advantages of secondary research are that it is relatively cheap and easily accessible.
   a. Market Research
   b. Mystery shoppers
   c. Questionnaire
   d. Mystery shopping

Chapter 5. Measuring Market Opportunities: Forecasting and Market Knowledge

20. _____ is the practice of individuals including commercial businesses, governments and institutions, facilitating the sale of their products or services to other companies or organizations that in turn resell them, use them as components in products or services they offer _____ is also called business-to-_____ for short. (Note that while marketing to government entities shares some of the same dynamics of organizational marketing, B2G Marketing is meaningfully different.)
    a. Business marketing
    b. Disruptive technology
    c. Law of disruption
    d. Mass marketing

21. _____ a research method involving the use of questionnaires and/or statistical surveys to gather data about people and their thoughts and behaviours.
    a. T-test
    b. Z-test
    c. Survey Research
    d. Control chart

22. The _____ is an English-language international daily newspaper published by Dow Jones ' Company in New York City with Asian and European editions. As of 2007, It has a worldwide daily circulation of more than 2 million, with approximately 931,000 paying online subscribers. It was the largest-circulation newspaper in the United States until November 2003, when it was surpassed by USA Today.
    a. Wall Street Journal
    b. 6-3-5 Brainwriting
    c. 180SearchAssistant
    d. Power III

23. _____ is a branch of philosophy which seeks to address questions about morality, such as how a moral outcome can be achieved in a specific situation (applied _____), how moral values should be determined (normative _____), what moral values people actually abide by (descriptive _____), what the fundamental semantic, ontological, and epistemic nature of _____ or morality is (meta-_____), and how moral capacity or moral agency develops and what its nature is (moral psychology.)

Socrates was one of the first Greek philosophers to encourage both scholars and the common citizen to turn their attention from the outside world to the condition of man. In this view, Knowledge having a bearing on human life was placed highest, all other knowledge being secondary.

a. AMAX
b. ADTECH
c. ACNielsen
d. Ethics

24. _____ is a set of six steps which defines the tasks to be accomplished in conducting a marketing research study. These include problem definition, developing an approach to problem, research design formulation, field work, data preparation and analysis, and report generation and presentation.
a. Market analysis
b. Marketing research process
c. Simple random sampling
d. Preference-rank translation

Chapter 6. Targeting Attractive Market Segments

1. A _____ is a subgroup of people or organizations sharing one or more characteristics that cause them to have similar product and/or service needs. A true _____ meets all of the following criteria: it is distinct from other segments (different segments have different needs), it is homogeneous within the segment (exhibits common needs); it responds similarly to a market stimulus, and it can be reached by a market intervention. The term is also used when consumers with identical product and/or service needs are divided up into groups so they can be charged different amounts.

    a. Production orientation
    b. Commercial planning
    c. Customer insight
    d. Market segment

2. _____ is defined by the American _____ Association as the activity, set of institutions, and processes for creating, communicating, delivering, and exchanging offerings that have value for customers, clients, partners, and society at large. The term developed from the original meaning which referred literally to going to market, as in shopping, or going to a market to sell goods or services.

    _____ practice tends to be seen as a creative industry, which includes advertising, distribution and selling.

    a. Product naming
    b. Marketing
    c. Customer acquisition management
    d. Marketing myopia

3. A _____ is a collection of symbols, experiences and associations connected with a product, a service, a person or any other artifact or entity.

    _____s have become increasingly important components of culture and the economy, now being described as 'cultural accessories and personal philosophies'.

    Some people distinguish the psychological aspect of a _____ from the experiential aspect.

    a. Brandable software
    b. Brand
    c. Brand equity
    d. Store brand

4. _____ is a broad label that refers to any individuals or households that use goods and services generated within the economy. The concept of a _____ is used in different contexts, so that the usage and significance of the term may vary.

    A _____ is a person who uses any product or service.

Chapter 6. Targeting Attractive Market Segments

   a. Consumer
   b. 180SearchAssistant
   c. 6-3-5 Brainwriting
   d. Power III

5. An _____ is a person who has possession of an enterprise and assumes significant accountability for the inherent risks and the outcome. It is an ambitious leader who combines land, labour, and capital to create and market new goods or services. The term is a loanword from French and was first defined by the Irish economist Richard Cantillon.
   a. AMAX
   b. ADTECH
   c. Entrepreneur
   d. ACNielsen

6. In environmental modeling and especially in hydrology, a _____ model means a model that is acceptably consistent with observed natural processes, i.e. that simulates well, for example, observed river discharge. It is a key concept of the so-called Generalized Likelihood Uncertainty Estimation (GLUE) methodology to quantify how uncertain environmental predictions are.
   a. 180SearchAssistant
   b. Power III
   c. Behavioral
   d. 6-3-5 Brainwriting

7. Its a tool for marketing. _____ is a multivariate statistical classification technique for discovering whether the individuals of a population fall into different groups by making quantitative comparisons of multiple characteristics with the assumption that the differences within any group should be less than the differences between groups.

The information technologies employed in _____ include geographic information system and database management software.

   a. Linear discriminant analysis
   b. Geodemographic segmentation
   c. Principal component analysis
   d. Multiple discriminant analysis

8. _____ refers to a business or organization attempting to acquire goods or services to accomplish the goals of the enterprise. Though there are several organizations that attempt to set standards in the _____ process, processes can vary greatly between organizations. Typically the word '_____' is not used interchangeably with the word 'procurement', since procurement typically includes Expediting, Supplier Quality, and Traffic and Logistics (T'L) in addition to _____.

a. Supply network
b. Supply chain
c. Drop shipping
d. Purchasing

9. The acronym _____, is a psychographic segmentation. It was developed in the 1970s to explain changing U.S. values and lifestyles. It has since been reworked to enhance its ability to predict consumer behavior.

According to the _____ Framework, groups of people are arranged in a rectangle and are based on two dimensions. The vertical dimension segments people based on the degree to which they are innovative and have resources such as income, education, self-confidence, intelligence, leadership skills, and energy.

a. Power III
b. 180SearchAssistant
c. 6-3-5 Brainwriting
d. VALS

10. _____ is a concept that denotes the precise probability of specific eventualities. Technically, the notion of _____ is independent from the notion of value and, as such, eventualities may have both beneficial and adverse consequences. However, in general usage the convention is to focus only on potential negative impact to some characteristic of value that may arise from a future event.

a. 6-3-5 Brainwriting
b. 180SearchAssistant
c. Power III
d. Risk

11. A _____ is a plan of action designed to achieve a particular goal.

_____ is different from tactics. In military terms, tactics is concerned with the conduct of an engagement while _____ is concerned with how different engagements are linked.

a. 180SearchAssistant
b. Power III
c. 6-3-5 Brainwriting
d. Strategy

Chapter 7. Differentiation and Positioning

1. In marketing, _____ has come to mean the process by which marketers try to create an image or identity in the minds of their target market for its product, brand, or organization. It is the 'relative competitive comparison' their product occupies in a given market as perceived by the target market.

Re-_____ involves changing the identity of a product, relative to the identity of competing products, in the collective minds of the target market.

  a. GE matrix
  b. Containerization
  c. Moratorium
  d. Positioning

2. The _____ is an English-language international daily newspaper published by Dow Jones ' Company in New York City with Asian and European editions. As of 2007, It has a worldwide daily circulation of more than 2 million, with approximately 931,000 paying online subscribers. It was the largest-circulation newspaper in the United States until November 2003, when it was surpassed by USA Today.
  a. 180SearchAssistant
  b. Power III
  c. 6-3-5 Brainwriting
  d. Wall Street Journal

3. In algebra, a _____ is a function depending on n that associates a scalar, det(A), to an n×n square matrix A. The fundamental geometric meaning of a _____ is a scale factor for measure when A is regarded as a linear transformation. _____s are important both in calculus, where they enter the substitution rule for several variables, and in multilinear algebra.

For a fixed nonnegative integer n, there is a unique _____ function for the n×n matrices over any commutative ring R. In particular, this function exists when R is the field of real or complex numbers.

  a. Motion Picture Association of America's film-rating system
  b. Black Friday
  c. Package-on-Package
  d. Determinant

4. Perceptual mapping is a graphics technique used by asset marketers that attempts to visually display the perceptions of customers or potential customers. Typically the position of a product, product line, brand, or company is displayed relative to their competition.

_____ can have any number of dimensions but the most common is two dimensions.

Chapter 7. Differentiation and Positioning

a. Developed country
b. Comparison-Shopping agent
c. Perceptual maps
d. Retail floor planning

5. A personal and cultural _____ is a relative ethic _____, an assumption upon which implementation can be extrapolated. A _____ system is a set of consistent _____s and measures that is soo not true. A principle _____ is a foundation upon which other _____s and measures of integrity are based.

a. Perceptual maps
b. Package-on-Package
c. Supreme Court of the United States
d. Value

6. _____ consists of the sale of goods or merchandise from a fixed location, such as a department store or kiosk in small or individual lots for direct consumption by the purchaser. _____ may include subordinated services, such as delivery. Purchasers may be individuals or businesses.

a. Retailing
b. Warehouse store
c. Charity shop
d. Thrifting

7. _____ is a statistical technique used in market research to determine how people value different features that make up an individual product or service.

The objective of _____ is to determine what combination of a limited number of attributes is most influential on respondent choice or decision making. A controlled set of potential products or services is shown to respondents and by analyzing how they make preferences between these products, the implicit valuation of the individual elements making up the product or service can be determined.

a. Conjoint analysis
b. Likert scale
c. Power III
d. Semantic differential

8. In the field of marketing, a customer _____ consists of the sum total of benefits which a vendor promises that a customer will receive in return for the customer's associated payment (or other value-transfer.)

Put simply, the _____ is what the customer gets for his money.

Accordingly, a customer can evaluate a company's value-proposition on two broad dimensions with multiple subsets:

1. relative performance: what the customer gets from the vendor relative to a competitor's offering;
2. price: which consists of the payment the customer makes to acquire the product or service; plus the access cost

The vendor-company's marketing and sales efforts offer a customer _____; the vendor-company's delivery and customer-service processes then fulfill that value-proposition.

A value-proposition can assist in a firm's marketing strategy, and may guide a business to target a particular market segment.

a. Marketing performance measurement and management
b. Relationship management
c. DefCom Australia
d. Value proposition

9. In algebra, the _____ of a polynomial with real or complex coefficients is a certain expression in the coefficients of the polynomial which is equal to zero if and only if the polynomial has a multiple root (i.e. a root with multiplicity greater than one) in the complex numbers. For example, the _____ of the quadratic polynomial

$$ax^2 + bx + c \text{ is } b^2 - 4ac.$$

The _____ of the cubic polynomial

$$ax^3 + bx^2 + cx + d \text{ is } b^2c^2 - 4ac^3 - 4b^3d - 27a^2d^2 + 18abcd.$$

a. Lifestyle center
b. Flighting
c. Discriminant
d. Consumption Map

10. Linear _____ and the related Fisher's linear discriminant are methods used in statistics and machine learning to find the linear combination of features which best separate two or more classes of objects or events. The resulting combination may be used as a linear classifier, or, more commonly, for dimensionality reduction before later classification.

LDiscriminant analysis is closely related to ANOVA (analysis of variance) and regression analysis, which also attempt to express one dependent variable as a linear combination of other features or measurements.

a. Multiple discriminant analysis
b. Geodemographic segmentation
c. Linear discriminant analysis
d. Discriminant analysis

11. _____ is a statistical method used to describe variability among observed variables in terms of fewer unobserved variables called factors. The observed variables are modeled as linear combinations of the factors, plus 'error' terms. The information gained about the interdependencies can be used later to reduce the set of variables in a dataset.
    a. Factor analysis
    b. Power III
    c. Semantic differential
    d. Likert scale

12. _____ is a set of related statistical techniques often used in information visualization for exploring similarities or dissimilarities in data. MDS is a special case of ordination. An MDS algorithm starts with a matrix of item-item similarities, then assigns a location to each item in N-dimensional space, where N is specified a priori.
    a. Situational theory of publics
    b. Convenience
    c. Cocooning
    d. Multidimensional scaling

13. _____ can be regarded as an outcome of mental processes (cognitive process) leading to the selection of a course of action among several alternatives. Every _____ process produces a final choice. The output can be an action or an opinion of choice.
    a. Decision making
    b. Power III
    c. 6-3-5 Brainwriting
    d. 180SearchAssistant

Chapter 8. Marketing Strategies for New Market Entries

1. Competitiveness is a comparative concept of the ability and performance of a firm, sub-sector or country to sell and supply goods and/or services in a given market. Although widely used in economics and business management, the usefulness of the concept, particularly in the context of national competitiveness, is vigorously disputed by economists, such as Paul Krugman.

The term may also be applied to markets, where it is used to refer to the extent to which the market structure may be regarded as perfectly _____.

   a. Free trade zone
   b. Geographical pricing
   c. Customs union
   d. Competitive

2. _____ is, in very basic words, a position a firm occupies against its competitors.

According to Michael Porter, the three methods for creating a sustainable _____ are through:

1. Cost leadership - Cost advantage occurs when a firm delivers the same services as its competitors but at a lower cost;

2.

   a. 6-3-5 Brainwriting
   b. Competitive advantage
   c. Power III
   d. 180SearchAssistant

3. A craze is a product, idea, cultural movement, or model that gains popularity among a small section of the populace then quickly migrates to the mainstream. Crazes are characterized by their lightning fast adoption and swift departure from public awareness. Crazes and _____s are also characterized by their unusually high interest and sales figures relative to the time they are active in the marketplace, as compared with other similar products, ideas, cultural movements or models.
   a. 180SearchAssistant
   b. 6-3-5 Brainwriting
   c. Power III
   d. Fad

4. _____ Management is the succession of strategies used by management as a product goes through its _____. The conditions in which a product is sold changes over time and must be managed as it moves through its succession of stages.

Chapter 8. Marketing Strategies for New Market Entries

The _____ goes through many phases, involves many professional disciplines, and requires many skills, tools and processes.

a. Chain stores
b. Supplier diversity
c. Customer satisfaction
d. Product life cycle

5. _____ is the pricing technique of setting a relatively low initial entry price, often lower than the eventual market price, to attract new customers. The strategy works on the expectation that customers will switch to the new brand because of the lower price. _____ is most commonly associated with a marketing objective of increasing market share or sales volume, rather than to make profit in the short term.

a. Price war
b. Fee
c. Competitor indexing
d. Penetration pricing

6. _____ is one of the four Ps of the marketing mix. The other three aspects are product, promotion, and place. It is also a key variable in microeconomic price allocation theory.

a. Competitor indexing
b. Pricing
c. Price
d. Relationship based pricing

7. _____ is one of the four elements of marketing mix. An organization or set of organizations (go-betweens) involved in the process of making a product or service available for use or consumption by a consumer or business user.

The other three parts of the marketing mix are product, pricing, and promotion.

a. Comparison-Shopping agent
b. Better Living Through Chemistry
c. Japan Advertising Photographers' Association
d. Distribution

Chapter 8. Marketing Strategies for New Market Entries

8. _____ involves disseminating information about a product, product line, brand, or company. It is one of the four key aspects of the marketing mix. (The other three elements are product marketing, pricing, and distribution). P>_____ is generally sub-divided into two parts:

- Above the line _____: Promotion in the media (e.g. TV, radio, newspapers, Internet and Mobile Phones) in which the advertiser pays an advertising agency to place the ad
- Below the line _____: All other _____. Much of this is intended to be subtle enough for the consumer to be unaware that _____ is taking place. E.g. sponsorship, product placement, endorsements, sales _____, merchandising, direct mail, personal selling, public relations, trade shows

a. Davie Brown Index
b. Promotion
c. Cashmere Agency
d. Bottling lines

9. _____ in economics and business is the result of an exchange and from that trade we assign a numerical monetary value to a good, service or asset. If I trade 4 apples for an orange, the _____ of an orange is 4 - apples. Inversely, the _____ of an apple is 1/4 oranges.

a. Discounts and allowances
b. Pricing
c. Contribution margin-based pricing
d. Price

10. In economics, business, retail, and accounting, a _____ is the value of money that has been used up to produce something, and hence is not available for use anymore. In economics, a _____ is an alternative that is given up as a result of a decision. In business, the _____ may be one of acquisition, in which case the amount of money expended to acquire it is counted as _____.

a. Transaction cost
b. Fixed costs
c. Variable cost
d. Cost

11. A _____ strategy targets non-buying customers in currently targeted segments. It also targets new customers in new segments. (Winer)

A marketing manager has to think about the following questions before implementing a _____ strategy: Is it profitable? Will it require the introduction of new or modified products? Is the customer and channel well enough researched and understood?

The marketing manager uses these four groups to give more focus to the market segment decision: existing customers, competitor customers, non-buying in current segments, new segments.

a. Market development
b. Commercial planning
c. Kano model
d. Perceptual mapping

12. In business and engineering, new _____ is the term used to describe the complete process of bringing a new product or service to market. There are two parallel paths involved in the Nproduct development process: one involves the idea generation, product design, and detail engineering; the other involves market research and marketing analysis. Companies typically see new _____ as the first stage in generating and commercializing new products within the overall strategic process of product life cycle management used to maintain or grow their market share.

a. New product screening
b. Product development
c. New product development
d. Specification tree

13. In economics, _____ is the desire to own something and the ability to pay for it. The term _____ signifies the ability or the willingness to buy a particular commodity at a given point of time .

a. Discretionary spending
b. Market system
c. Demand
d. Market dominance

14. A _____ is a plan of action designed to achieve a particular goal.

_____ is different from tactics. In military terms, tactics is concerned with the conduct of an engagement while _____ is concerned with how different engagements are linked.

a. 6-3-5 Brainwriting
b. Strategy
c. Power III
d. 180SearchAssistant

Chapter 8. Marketing Strategies for New Market Entries

15. Procter is a surname, and may also refer to:

- Bryan Waller Procter (pseud. Barry Cornwall), English poet
- Goodwin Procter, American law firm
- _____, consumer products multinational

a. Black PRies
b. Flyer
c. Convergent
d. Procter ' Gamble

16. _____ is defined by the American _____ Association as the activity, set of institutions, and processes for creating, communicating, delivering, and exchanging offerings that have value for customers, clients, partners, and society at large. The term developed from the original meaning which referred literally to going to market, as in shopping, or going to a market to sell goods or services.

_____ practice tends to be seen as a creative industry, which includes advertising, distribution and selling.

a. Product naming
b. Customer acquisition management
c. Marketing
d. Marketing myopia

17. A _____ is defined by the International Co-operative Alliance's Statement on the Co-operative Identity as an autonomous association of persons united voluntarily to meet their common economic, social, and cultural needs and aspirations through a jointly-owned and democratically-controlled enterprise. It is a business organization owned and operated by a group of individuals for their mutual benefit. A _____ may also be defined as a business owned and controlled equally by the people who use its services or who work at it.

a. Cooperative
b. 6-3-5 Brainwriting
c. Power III
d. 180SearchAssistant

18. In economics, an _____ is any good or commodity, transported from one country to another country in a legitimate fashion, typically for use in trade. _____ goods or services are provided to foreign consumers by domestic producers. _____ is an important part of international trade.

a. ACNielsen
b. ADTECH
c. AMAX
d. Export

19. _____ is exchange of capital, goods, and services across international borders or territories. In most countries, it represents a significant share of gross domestic product (GDP.) While _____ has been present throughout much of history, its economic, social, and political importance has been on the rise in recent centuries.

a. Incoterms
b. International trade
c. ADTECH
d. ACNielsen

20. _____s function as professionals who deal with trade, dealing in commodities that they do not produce themselves, in order to produce profit.

_____s can be of two types:

1. A wholesale _____ operates in the chain between producer and retail _____. Some wholesale _____s only organize the movement of goods rather than move the goods themselves.
2. A retail _____ or retailer, sells commodities to consumers (including businesses.) A shop owner is a retail _____.

A _____ class characterizes many pre-modern societies. Its status can range from high (even achieving titles like that of _____ prince or nabob) to low, such as in Chinese culture, due to the soiling capabilities of profiting from 'mere' trade, rather than from the labor of others reflected in agricultural produce, craftsmanship, and tribute.

In the United States, '_____' is defined (under the Uniform Commercial Code) as any person while engaged in a business or profession or a seller who deals regularly in the type of goods sold.

a. RFM
b. Trade credit
c. Retail loss prevention
d. Merchant

Chapter 8. Marketing Strategies for New Market Entries

21. _____ is the practice of individuals including commercial businesses, governments and institutions, facilitating the sale of their products or services to other companies or organizations that in turn resell them, use them as components in products or services they offer _____ is also called business-to-_____ for short. (Note that while marketing to government entities shares some of the same dynamics of organizational marketing, B2G Marketing is meaningfully different.)
    a. Disruptive technology
    b. Law of disruption
    c. Mass marketing
    d. Business marketing

22. A _____ is a firm that manufactures components or products for another 'hiring' firm. Many industries utilize this process, especially the aerospace, defense, computer, semiconductor, energy, medical, food manufacturing, personal care, and automotive fields. Some types of contract manufacturing include CNC machining, complex assembly, aluminum die casting, grinding, broaching, gears, and forging.
    a. Power III
    b. Contract manufacturer
    c. 180SearchAssistant
    d. Productivity

23. The most important feature of a contract is that one party makes an _____ for an arrangement that another accepts. This can be called a 'concurrence of wills' or 'ad idem' (meeting of the minds) of two or more parties. The concept is somewhat contested.
    a. ADTECH
    b. ACNielsen
    c. AMAX
    d. Offer

24. _____ is exchanging goods or services that are paid for, in whole or part, with other goods or services.

There are five main variants of _____:

- Barter: Exchange of goods or services directly for other goods or services without the use of money as means of purchase or payment.
- Switch trading: Practice in which one company sells to another its obligation to make a purchase in a given country.
- Counter purchase: Sale of goods and services to a country by a company that promises to make a future purchase of a specific product from the country.
- Buyback: occurs when a firm builds a plant in a country - or supplies technology, equipment, training, or other services to the country and agrees to take a certain percentage of the plant's output as partial payment for the contract.
- Offset: Agreement that a company will offset a hard - currency purchase of an unspecified product from that nation in the future. Agreement by one nation to buy a product from another, subject to the purchase of some or all of the components and raw materials from the buyer of the finished product, or the assembly of such product in the buyer nation.

a. Merchant
b. Retail loss prevention
c. RFM
d. Countertrade

25. _____ refers to the methods of practicing and using another person's philosophy of business. The franchisor grants the independent operator the right to distribute its products, techniques, and trademarks for a percentage of gross monthly sales and a royalty fee. Various tangibles and intangibles such as national or international advertising, training, and other support services are commonly made available by the franchisor.

a. Franchise fee
b. Franchising
c. 180SearchAssistant
d. Power III

26. A _____ is an entity formed between two or more parties to undertake economic activity together. The parties agree to create a new entity by both contributing equity, and they then share in the revenues, expenses, and control of the enterprise. The venture can be for one specific project only, or a continuing business relationship such as the Fuji Xerox _____.

a. Gripe site
b. Trademark attorney
c. Consumer protection
d. Joint venture

27. The verb _____ or grant _____ means to give permission. The noun _____ refers to that permission as well as to the document memorializing that permission. _____ may be granted by a party to another party as an element of an agreement between those parties.

   a. License
   b. 180SearchAssistant
   c. 6-3-5 Brainwriting
   d. Power III

28. Foreign _____ in its classic form is defined as a company from one country making a physical investment into building a factory in another country. It is the establishment of an enterprise by a foreigner. Its definition can be extended to include investments made to acquire lasting interest in enterprises operating outside of the economy of the investor.

   a. Fountain Fresh International
   b. Brash Brands
   c. VideoJug
   d. Direct investment

29. _____ is the state or fact of exclusive rights and control over property, which may be an object, land/real estate, or some other kind of property (like government-granted monopolies collectively referred to as intellectual property.) It is embodied in an _____ right also referred to as title.

   _____ is the key building block in the development of the capitalist socio-economic system.

   a. AMAX
   b. Ownership
   c. ACNielsen
   d. ADTECH

Chapter 9. Strategies for Growth Markets

1. _____ is a concept that denotes the precise probability of specific eventualities. Technically, the notion of _____ is independent from the notion of value and, as such, eventualities may have both beneficial and adverse consequences. However, in general usage the convention is to focus only on potential negative impact to some characteristic of value that may arise from a future event.
    a. 180SearchAssistant
    b. 6-3-5 Brainwriting
    c. Risk
    d. Power III

2. A _____ is a plan of action designed to achieve a particular goal.

    _____ is different from tactics. In military terms, tactics is concerned with the conduct of an engagement while _____ is concerned with how different engagements are linked.

    a. Power III
    b. Strategy
    c. 6-3-5 Brainwriting
    d. 180SearchAssistant

3. A _____ is a collection of symbols, experiences and associations connected with a product, a service, a person or any other artifact or entity.

    _____s have become increasingly important components of culture and the economy, now being described as 'cultural accessories and personal philosophies'.

    Some people distinguish the psychological aspect of a _____ from the experiential aspect.

    a. Brandable software
    b. Brand equity
    c. Store brand
    d. Brand

Chapter 10. Strategies for Mature and Declining Markets

1. _____ is an advertisement in which a particular product specifically mentions a competitor by name for the express purpose of showing why the competitor is inferior to the product naming it.

This should not be confused with parody advertisements, where a fictional product is being advertised for the purpose of poking fun at the particular advertisement, nor should it be confused with the use of a coined brand name for the purpose of comparing the product without actually naming an actual competitor. ('Wikipedia tastes better and is less filling than the Encyclopedia Galactica.')

In the 1980s, during what has been referred to as the cola wars, soft-drink manufacturer Pepsi ran a series of advertisements where people, caught on hidden camera, in a blind taste test, chose Pepsi over rival Coca-Cola.

   a. GL-70
   b. Cost per conversion
   c. Heavy-up
   d. Comparative advertising

2. A _____ is a collection of symbols, experiences and associations connected with a product, a service, a person or any other artifact or entity.

_____s have become increasingly important components of culture and the economy, now being described as 'cultural accessories and personal philosophies'.

Some people distinguish the psychological aspect of a _____ from the experiential aspect.

   a. Brand
   b. Brand equity
   c. Store brand
   d. Brandable software

3. A _____ is an explicit set of requirements to be satisfied by a material, product, or service.

In engineering, manufacturing, and business, it is vital for suppliers, purchasers, and users of materials, products, or services to understand and agree upon all requirements. A _____ is a type of a standard which is often referenced by a contract or procurement document.

   a. Product development
   b. Product optimization
   c. Specification
   d. New product development

Chapter 10. Strategies for Mature and Declining Markets

4. In psychology, philosophy, and the cognitive sciences, _____ is the process of attaining awareness or understanding of sensory information. It is a task far more complex than was imagined in the 1950s and 1960s, when it was predicted that building perceiving machines would take about a decade, a goal which is still very far from fruition. The word _____ comes from the Latin words _____, percepio, meaning 'receiving, collecting, action of taking possession, apprehension with the mind or senses.'

_____ is one of the oldest fields in psychology.

   a. 180SearchAssistant
   b. Perception
   c. Groupthink
   d. Power III

5. _____ is a term used to describe any service or product for which the non-essential features have been removed. The use of the term 'frills' refers to a style of fabric decoration. Something offered to customers for no additional charge may be designated as a 'frill' - for example, free drinks on airline journeys, or a radio installed in a rental car.
   a. 6-3-5 Brainwriting
   b. Power III
   c. No frills
   d. 180SearchAssistant

6. _____ can be defined as the idea generation, concept development, testing and manufacturing or implementation of a physical object or service. _____ers conceptualize and evaluate ideas, making them tangible through products in a more systematic approach. The role of a _____er encompasses many characteristics of the marketing manager, product manager, industrial designer and design engineer.
   a. African Americans
   b. Albert Einstein
   c. AStore
   d. Product design

7. A _____ is something that is acted upon or used by or by human labour or industry, for use as a building material to create some product or structure. Often the term is used to denote material that came from nature and is in an unprocessed or minimally processed state. Iron ore, logs, and crude oil, would be examples.
   a. 6-3-5 Brainwriting
   b. 180SearchAssistant
   c. Power III
   d. Raw material

Chapter 10. Strategies for Mature and Declining Markets

8. _____ is one of the four elements of marketing mix. An organization or set of organizations (go-betweens) involved in the process of making a product or service available for use or consumption by a consumer or business user.

The other three parts of the marketing mix are product, pricing, and promotion.

a. Comparison-Shopping agent
b. Japan Advertising Photographers' Association
c. Distribution
d. Better Living Through Chemistry

9. _____, a business term, is a measure of how products and services supplied by a company meet or surpass customer expectation. It is seen as a key performance indicator within business and is part of the four perspectives of a Balanced Scorecard.

In a competitive marketplace where businesses compete for customers, _____ is seen as a key differentiator and increasingly has become a key element of business strategy.

a. Psychological pricing
b. Customer satisfaction
c. Supplier diversity
d. Customer base

10. _____ is defined by the American _____ Association as the activity, set of institutions, and processes for creating, communicating, delivering, and exchanging offerings that have value for customers, clients, partners, and society at large. The term developed from the original meaning which referred literally to going to market, as in shopping, or going to a market to sell goods or services.

_____ practice tends to be seen as a creative industry, which includes advertising, distribution and selling.

a. Marketing
b. Customer acquisition management
c. Product naming
d. Marketing myopia

11. A _____ is a process that can allow an organization to concentrate its limited resources on the greatest opportunities to increase sales and achieve a sustainable competitive advantage. A _____ should be centered around the key concept that customer satisfaction is the main goal.

A _____ is most effective when it is an integral component of corporate strategy, defining how the organization will successfully engage customers, prospects, and competitors in the market arena.

Chapter 10. Strategies for Mature and Declining Markets

a. Psychographic
b. Societal marketing
c. Cyberdoc
d. Marketing strategy

12. A _____ is a plan of action designed to achieve a particular goal.

_____ is different from tactics. In military terms, tactics is concerned with the conduct of an engagement while _____ is concerned with how different engagements are linked.

a. 6-3-5 Brainwriting
b. 180SearchAssistant
c. Power III
d. Strategy

13. _____ is the study of the Earth and its lands, features, inhabitants, and phenomena. A literal translation would be 'to describe or write about the Earth'. The first person to use the word '_____' was Eratosthenes .

a. 180SearchAssistant
b. Power III
c. 6-3-5 Brainwriting
d. Geography

14. Competitiveness is a comparative concept of the ability and performance of a firm, sub-sector or country to sell and supply goods and/or services in a given market. Although widely used in economics and business management, the usefulness of the concept, particularly in the context of national competitiveness, is vigorously disputed by economists, such as Paul Krugman .

The term may also be applied to markets, where it is used to refer to the extent to which the market structure may be regarded as perfectly _____.

a. Free trade zone
b. Geographical pricing
c. Customs union
d. Competitive

Chapter 10. Strategies for Mature and Declining Markets

15. In economics, _____ is the desire to own something and the ability to pay for it. The term _____ signifies the ability or the willingness to buy a particular commodity at a given point of time .

a. Discretionary spending
b. Market dominance
c. Market system
d. Demand

16. _____ is a measure of the strength of a brand, product, service relative to competitive offerings. There is often a geographic element to the competitive landscape. In defining _____, you must see to what extent a product, brand, or firm controls a product category in a given geographic area.

a. Market system
b. Discretionary spending
c. Productivity
d. Market dominance

Chapter 11. Marketing Strategies for the New Economy

1. _____ is a virtual world developed by Linden Lab that launched on June 23, 2003 and is accessible via the Internet. A free client program called the _____ Viewer enables its users, called Residents, to interact with each other through avatars. Residents can explore, meet other residents, socialize, participate in individual and group activities, and create and trade virtual property and services with one another, or travel throughout the world, which residents refer to as the grid.
    a. Complex sale
    b. Second Life
    c. Promotion
    d. Relationship Management Application

2. _____ is an independent technology and market research company that provides its clients with advice about technology's impact on business and consumers. _____ has four research centers in the US: Cambridge, Massachusetts; Foster City, California; Washington, D.C.; and Westport, Connecticut. It also has four European research centers in Amsterdam, Frankfurt, London, and Paris.
    a. Mapinfo
    b. BigMachines
    c. Forrester Research
    d. GlobalSpec

3. Electronic commerce, commonly known as _____ or eCommerce, consists of the buying and selling of products or services over electronic systems such as the Internet and other computer networks. The amount of trade conducted electronically has grown extraordinarily with wide-spread Internet usage. A wide variety of commerce is conducted in this way, spurring and drawing on innovations in electronic funds transfer, supply chain management, Internet marketing, online transaction processing, electronic data interchange (EDI), inventory management systems, and automated data collection systems.
    a. ADTECH
    b. ACNielsen
    c. AMAX
    d. E-commerce

4. _____ is one of the four elements of marketing mix. An organization or set of organizations (go-betweens) involved in the process of making a product or service available for use or consumption by a consumer or business user.

    The other three parts of the marketing mix are product, pricing, and promotion.

    a. Distribution
    b. Japan Advertising Photographers' Association
    c. Better Living Through Chemistry
    d. Comparison-Shopping agent

5. In calculus, a function f defined on a subset of the real numbers with real values is called _____, if for all x and y such that x ≤ y one has f(x) ≤ f(y), so f preserves the order. In layman's terms, the sign of the slope is always positive (the curve tending upwards) or zero (i.e., non-decreasing, or asymptotic, or depicted as a horizontal, flat line) Likewise, a function is called monotonically decreasing (non-increasing) if, whenever x ≤ y, then f(x) ≥ f(y), so it reverses the order.
   a. 180SearchAssistant
   b. 6-3-5 Brainwriting
   c. Power III
   d. Monotonic

6. _____ is a recursive process where two or more people or organizations work together toward an intersection of common goals -- for example, an intellectual endeavor that is creative in nature--by sharing knowledge, learning and building consensus. _____ does not require leadership and can sometimes bring better results through decentralization and egalitarianism. In particular, teams that work collaboratively can obtain greater resources, recognition and reward when facing competition for finite resources. _____ is also present in opposing goals exhibiting the notion of adversarial _____, though this notion is atypical of the annotation that people have given towards their understanding of _____.
   a. 180SearchAssistant
   b. 6-3-5 Brainwriting
   c. Power III
   d. Collaboration

7. _____ is the process of filtering for information or patterns using techniques involving collaboration among multiple agents, viewpoints, data sources, etc. Applications of _____ typically involve very large data sets. _____ methods have been applied to many different kinds of data including sensing and monitoring data - such as in mineral exploration, environmental sensing over large areas or multiple sensors; financial data - such as financial service institutions that integrate many financial sources; or in electronic commerce and web 2.0 applications where the focus is on user data, etc.
   a. Power III
   b. 6-3-5 Brainwriting
   c. 180SearchAssistant
   d. Collaborative filtering

8. On an intranet or B2E Enterprise Web portals, personalization is often based on user attributes such as department, functional area, or role. The term _____ in this context refers to the ability of users to modify the page layout or specify what content should be displayed.

Chapter 11. Marketing Strategies for the New Economy

There are two categories of personalizations:

1. Rule-based
2. Content-based

Web personalization models include rules-based filtering, based on 'if this, then that' rules processing, and collaborative filtering, which serves relevant material to customers by combining their own personal preferences with the preferences of like-minded others. Collaborative filtering works well for books, music, video, etc.

a. Cashmere Agency
b. Movin'
c. Customization
d. Self branding

9. _____ or personalisation is tailoring a consumer product, electronic or written medium to a user based on personal details or characteristics they provide. More recently, it has especially been applied in the context of the World Wide Web.

Web pages are personalized based on the interests of an individual.

a. Flighting
b. Complex sale
c. Sexism,
d. Personalization

10. In economics, _____ is the removal of intermediaries in a supply chain: 'cutting out the middleman'. Instead of going through traditional distribution channels, which had some type of intermediate (such as a distributor, wholesaler, broker, or agent), companies may now deal with every customer directly, for example via the Internet. One important factor is a drop in the cost of servicing customers directly.
a. Social shopping
b. Spamvertising
c. Consumer-to-consumer
d. Disintermediation

11. A _____ is a plan of action designed to achieve a particular goal.

_____ is different from tactics. In military terms, tactics is concerned with the conduct of an engagement while _____ is concerned with how different engagements are linked.

a. Power III
b. Strategy
c. 180SearchAssistant
d. 6-3-5 Brainwriting

12. _____ is the advantage gained by the initial occupant of a market segment. This advantage may stem from the fact that the first entrant can gain control of resources that followers may not be able to match. Sometimes the first mover is not able to capitalise on its advantage, leaving the opportunity for another firm to gain second-mover advantage.

a. Business stature
b. Time to market
c. Psychological pricing
d. First-mover advantage

13. _____ is a broad label that refers to any individuals or households that use goods and services generated within the economy. The concept of a _____ is used in different contexts, so that the usage and significance of the term may vary.

A _____ is a person who uses any product or service.

a. 6-3-5 Brainwriting
b. Power III
c. 180SearchAssistant
d. Consumer

14. _____ is the collection, deployment and translation of information that allows a business to acquire, develop and retain their customers.

Firslty, the collected data must be audited to fully understand the quality and opportunity within the database. Once this is done, there are a number of different types of analysis that can be applied.

a. Societal marketing
b. Fifth screen
c. Customer analytics
d. Customer insight

Chapter 11. Marketing Strategies for the New Economy

15. _____ involves disseminating information about a product, product line, brand, or company. It is one of the four key aspects of the marketing mix. (The other three elements are product marketing, pricing, and distribution). P>_____ is generally sub-divided into two parts:

- Above the line _____: Promotion in the media (e.g. TV, radio, newspapers, Internet and Mobile Phones) in which the advertiser pays an advertising agency to place the ad
- Below the line _____: All other _____. Much of this is intended to be subtle enough for the consumer to be unaware that _____ is taking place. E.g. sponsorship, product placement, endorsements, sales _____, merchandising, direct mail, personal selling, public relations, trade shows

a. Promotion
b. Bottling lines
c. Cashmere Agency
d. Davie Brown Index

16. A _____ is a collection of symbols, experiences and associations connected with a product, a service, a person or any other artifact or entity.

_____s have become increasingly important components of culture and the economy, now being described as 'cultural accessories and personal philosophies'.

Some people distinguish the psychological aspect of a _____ from the experiential aspect.

a. Brandable software
b. Store brand
c. Brand equity
d. Brand

17. _____ is an advertisement in which a particular product specifically mentions a competitor by name for the express purpose of showing why the competitor is inferior to the product naming it.

This should not be confused with parody advertisements, where a fictional product is being advertised for the purpose of poking fun at the particular advertisement, nor should it be confused with the use of a coined brand name for the purpose of comparing the product without actually naming an actual competitor. ('Wikipedia tastes better and is less filling than the Encyclopedia Galactica.')

In the 1980s, during what has been referred to as the cola wars, soft-drink manufacturer Pepsi ran a series of advertisements where people, caught on hidden camera, in a blind taste test, chose Pepsi over rival Coca-Cola.

Chapter 11. Marketing Strategies for the New Economy

a. GL-70
b. Comparative advertising
c. Cost per conversion
d. Heavy-up

18. _____ is defined by the American _____ Association as the activity, set of institutions, and processes for creating, communicating, delivering, and exchanging offerings that have value for customers, clients, partners, and society at large. The term developed from the original meaning which referred literally to going to market, as in shopping, or going to a market to sell goods or services.

_____ practice tends to be seen as a creative industry, which includes advertising, distribution and selling.

a. Product naming
b. Marketing myopia
c. Customer acquisition management
d. Marketing

19. Consumer market research is a form of applied sociology that concentrates on understanding the behaviours, whims and preferences, of consumers in a market-based economy, and aims to understand the effects and comparative success of marketing campaigns. The field of consumer _____ as a statistical science was pioneered by Arthur Nielsen with the founding of the ACNielsen Company in 1923 .

Thus _____ is the systematic and objective identification, collection, analysis, and dissemination of information for the purpose of assisting management in decision making related to the identification and solution of problems and opportunities in marketing.

a. Marketing research process
b. Marketing research
c. Logit analysis
d. Focus group

20. _____, also referred to as i-marketing, web marketing, online marketing is the marketing of products or services over the Internet.

The Internet has brought many unique benefits to marketing, one of which being lower costs for the distribution of information and media to a global audience. The interactive nature of _____, both in terms of providing instant response and eliciting responses, is a unique quality of the medium.

a. AMAX
b. ADTECH
c. ACNielsen
d. Internet marketing

21. A _____ is a type of website, usually maintained by an individual with regular entries of commentary, descriptions of events, or other material such as graphics or video. Entries are commonly displayed in reverse-chronological order. '_____' can also be used as a verb, meaning to maintain or add content to a _____.

   a. Power III
   b. Blog
   c. 6-3-5 Brainwriting
   d. 180SearchAssistant

22. _____ is a form of direct marketing which uses electronic mail as a means of communicating commercial or fundraising messages to an audience. In its broadest sense, every e-mail sent to a potential or current customer could be considered _____. However, the term is usually used to refer to:

   - sending e-mails with the purpose of enhancing the relationship of a merchant with its current or previous customers and to encourage customer loyalty and repeat business,
   - sending e-mails with the purpose of acquiring new customers or convincing current customers to purchase something immediately,
   - adding advertisements to e-mails sent by other companies to their customers, and
   - sending e-mails over the Internet, as e-mail did and does exist outside the Internet (e.g., network e-mail and FIDO.)

Researchers estimate that United States firms alone spent US$400 million on _____ in 2006.

Chapter 11. Marketing Strategies for the New Economy

_____ is popular with companies for several reasons:

- A mailing list provides the ability to distribute information to a wide range of specific, potential customers at a relatively low cost.
- Compared to other media investments such as direct mail or printed newsletters, e-mail is less expensive.
- An exact return on investment can be tracked ('track to basket') and has proven to be high when done properly. _____ is often reported as second only to search marketing as the most effective online marketing tactic.
- The delivery time for an e-mail message is short (i.e., seconds or minutes) as compared to a mailed advertisement (i.e., one or more days.)
- An advertiser is able to 'push' the message to its audience, as opposed to website-based advertising, which relies on a customer to visit that website.
- It is possible to impress the target audience using various unique fonts and formats. This will help in making the email messages more appealing and sweet.
- E-mail messages are easy to track. An advertiser can track users via autoresponders, web bugs, bounce messages, unsubscribe requests, read receipts, click-throughs, etc. These mechanisms can be used to measure open rates, positive or negative responses, and to correlate sales with marketing.
- Advertisers can generate repeat business affordably and automatically.
- Advertisers can reach substantial numbers of e-mail subscribers who have opted in (i.e., consented) to receive e-mail communications on subjects of interest to them.
- Over half of Internet users check or send e-mail on a typical day.
- Specific types of interaction with messages can trigger (1) other messages to be delivered automatically, or (2) other events, such as updating the profile of the recipient to indicate a specific interest category.
- _____ is paper-free (i.e., 'green'.)

Many companies use _____ to communicate with existing customers, but many other companies send unsolicited bulk e-mail, also known as spam.

Internet system administrators have always considered themselves responsible for dealing with 'abuse of the net', but not 'abuse on the net'.

a. Enterprise Search Marketing
b. Online shopping rewards
c. Audience Screening
d. E-mail marketing

23. _____ is a search engine marketing product where the search engine company charges fees related to inclusion of websites in their search index. _____ products are provided by most search engine companies, the most notable exception being Google.

Chapter 11. Marketing Strategies for the New Economy 65

a. Paid inclusion
b. Hit inflation attack
c. Microsoft adCenter
d. VoloMedia

24. _____ is the process of improving the volume and quality of traffic to a web site from search engines via 'natural' ('organic' or 'algorithmic') search results. Typically, the earlier a site appears in the search results list, the more visitors it will receive from the search engine. _____ may target different kinds of search, including image search, local search, and industry-specific vertical search engines.

a. 6-3-5 Brainwriting
b. 180SearchAssistant
c. Power III
d. Search engine optimization

25. _____ is a term used in marketing in general and e-marketing specifically. Marketers will ask permission before advancing to the next step in the purchasing process. For example, they ask permission to send advertisements to prospective customers.

a. Spam Lit
b. Personalized marketing
c. Live banner
d. Permission marketing

26. Procter is a surname, and may also refer to:

- Bryan Waller Procter (pseud. Barry Cornwall), English poet
- Goodwin Procter, American law firm
- _____, consumer products multinational

a. Flyer
b. Convergent
c. Procter ' Gamble
d. Black PRies

27. _____, sometimes referred to as information richness theory, is a framework that can be used to describe a communications medium by describing its ability to reproduce the information sent over it. It was developed by Richard L. Daft and Robert H. Lengel. For example, a phone call will not be able to reproduce visual social cues such as gestures.

Chapter 11. Marketing Strategies for the New Economy

a. 180SearchAssistant
b. Media richness theory
c. 6-3-5 Brainwriting
d. Power III

28. _____ is a form of communication that typically attempts to persuade potential customers to purchase or to consume more of a particular brand of product or service. 'While now central to the contemporary global economy and the reproduction of global production networks, it is only quite recently that _____ has been more than a marginal influence on patterns of sales and production. The formation of modern _____ was intimately bound up with the emergence of new forms of monopoly capitalism around the end of the 19th and beginning of the 20th century as one element in corporate strategies to create, organize and where possible control markets, especially for mass produced consumer goods.
   a. AMAX
   b. ACNielsen
   c. ADTECH
   d. Advertising

29. Why do retail stores need _____? With respect to the key objectives of growth and profit for any retail entity, _____ should significantly improve sales margins and increase sales by enabling the vendor to price variably and hence suitably and to control its product range based on profit margins. The retail stores will be able to compete more effectively with rivals in the form of mixed multiples, mail order and online retailers, who are often able to undercut but who do not generally have the same understanding of the retail market. In particular _____ is recognised as encouraging impulse buys, cross-selling of products and repeat sales.
   a. Power III
   b. 180SearchAssistant
   c. 6-3-5 Brainwriting
   d. Dynamic pricing

30. _____ is one of the four Ps of the marketing mix. The other three aspects are product, promotion, and place. It is also a key variable in microeconomic price allocation theory.
   a. Competitor indexing
   b. Pricing
   c. Price
   d. Relationship based pricing

31. _____ is the activity that the selling organization undertakes to reduce customer account defections. The success of this activity is when the customer account places an additional order before a 12-month period has expired. Note that ideally these orders will need to contribute similar financial amounts to the previous 12 months.

a. Customer centricity
b. First-mover advantage
c. Customer base
d. Customer retention

32. An _____ is the manufacturing of a good or service within a category. Although _____ is a broad term for any kind of economic production, in economics and urban planning _____ is a synonym for the secondary sector, which is a type of economic activity involved in the manufacturing of raw materials into goods and products.

There are four key industrial economic sectors: the primary sector, largely raw material extraction industries such as mining and farming; the secondary sector, involving refining, construction, and manufacturing; the tertiary sector, which deals with services (such as law and medicine) and distribution of manufactured goods; and the quaternary sector, a relatively new type of knowledge _____ focusing on technological research, design and development such as computer programming, and biochemistry.

a. Industry
b. ADTECH
c. ACNielsen
d. AMAX

33. _____ is a social networking website with an interactive, user-submitted network of friends, personal profiles, blogs, groups, photos, music, and videos for teenagers and adults internationally. Its headquarters are in Beverly Hills, California, USA, where it shares an office building with its immediate owner, Fox Interactive Media; which is owned by News Corporation, which has its headquarters in New York City. In June 2006, _____ was the most popular social networking site in the United States.

a. Chief marketing officer
b. National Asset Recovery Services
c. Fountain Fresh International
d. MySpace

Chapter 12. Organizing and Planning for Effective Implementation

1. Competitiveness is a comparative concept of the ability and performance of a firm, sub-sector or country to sell and supply goods and/or services in a given market. Although widely used in economics and business management, the usefulness of the concept, particularly in the context of national competitiveness, is vigorously disputed by economists, such as Paul Krugman .

The term may also be applied to markets, where it is used to refer to the extent to which the market structure may be regarded as perfectly _____.

   a. Competitive
   b. Geographical pricing
   c. Customs union
   d. Free trade zone

2. _____ is the realization of an application idea, model, design, specification, standard, algorithm an _____ is a realization of a technical specification or algorithm as a program, software component, or other computer system. Many _____s may exist for a given specification or standard.

   a. AMAX
   b. ADTECH
   c. ACNielsen
   d. Implementation

3. A _____ is a plan of action designed to achieve a particular goal.

_____ is different from tactics. In military terms, tactics is concerned with the conduct of an engagement while _____ is concerned with how different engagements are linked.

   a. 6-3-5 Brainwriting
   b. 180SearchAssistant
   c. Strategy
   d. Power III

4. _____ is systematic determination of merit, worth, and significance of something or someone using criteria against a set of standards. _____ often is used to characterize and appraise subjects of interest in a wide range of human enterprises, including the arts, criminal justice, foundations and non-profit organizations, government, health care, and other human services.

Depending on the topic of interest, there are professional groups which look to the quality and rigor of the _____ process.

Chapter 12. Organizing and Planning for Effective Implementation

a. ADTECH
b. Evaluation
c. ACNielsen
d. AMAX

5. _____s is the social science that studies the production, distribution, and consumption of goods and services. The term _____s comes from the Ancient Greek οἰκονομία from οἶκος (oikos, 'house') + νόμος (nomos, 'custom' or 'law'), hence 'rules of the house(hold)'. Current _____ models developed out of the broader field of political economy in the late 19th century, owing to a desire to use an empirical approach more akin to the physical sciences.
   a. ACNielsen
   b. Industrial organization
   c. ADTECH
   d. Economic

6. The _____ of a good or service has puzzled economists since the beginning of the discipline. First, economists tried to estimate the value of a good to an individual alone, and extend that definition to goods which can be exchanged. From this analysis came the concepts value in use and value in exchange.
   a. ACNielsen
   b. ADTECH
   c. AMAX
   d. Economic value

7. A personal and cultural _____ is a relative ethic _____, an assumption upon which implementation can be extrapolated. A _____ system is a set of consistent _____s and measures that is soo not true. A principle _____ is a foundation upon which other _____s and measures of integrity are based.
   a. Supreme Court of the United States
   b. Package-on-Package
   c. Perceptual maps
   d. Value

8. _____ refers to the additional value of a commodity over the cost of commodities used to produce it from the previous stage of production. An example is the price of gasoline at the pump over the price of the oil in it. In national accounts used in macroeconomics, it refers to the contribution of the factors of production, i.e., land, labor, and capital goods, to raising the value of a product and corresponds to the incomes received by the owners of these factors. The factors of production provide 'services' which raise the unit price of a product (X) relative to the cost per unit of intermediate goods used up in the production of X. _____ is shared between the factors of production (capital, labor, also human capital), giving rise to issues of distribution.

Chapter 12. Organizing and Planning for Effective Implementation

a. Deregulation
b. Value added
c. Power III
d. Consumer spending

9. _____ is the practice of individuals including commercial businesses, governments and institutions, facilitating the sale of their products or services to other companies or organizations that in turn resell them, use them as components in products or services they offer _____ is also called business-to-_____ for short. (Note that while marketing to government entities shares some of the same dynamics of organizational marketing, B2G Marketing is meaningfully different.)

a. Disruptive technology
b. Business marketing
c. Law of disruption
d. Mass marketing

10. _____ is an organizational lifecycle function within a company dealing with the planning or marketing of a product or products at all stages of the product lifecycle.

_____ and product marketing (outbound focused) are different yet complementary efforts with the objective of maximizing sales revenues, market share, and profit margins. The role of _____ spans many activities from strategic to tactical and varies based on the organizational structure of the company.

a. Product information management
b. Service product management
c. Requirement prioritization
d. Product management

11. A _____ is an entity formed between two or more parties to undertake economic activity together. The parties agree to create a new entity by both contributing equity, and they then share in the revenues, expenses, and control of the enterprise. The venture can be for one specific project only, or a continuing business relationship such as the Fuji Xerox _____.

a. Joint venture
b. Consumer protection
c. Trademark attorney
d. Gripe site

12. A _____ or subscription radio is a digital radio signal that is broadcast by a communications satellite, which covers a much wider geographical range than terrestrial radio signals.

Chapter 12. Organizing and Planning for Effective Implementation

For now, _____ offers a meaningful alternative to ground-based radio services in some countries, notably the United States. Mobile services, such as Sirius, XM, and Worldspace, allow listeners to roam across an entire continent, listening to the same audio programming anywhere they go.

a. Power III
b. 6-3-5 Brainwriting
c. Satellite Radio
d. 180SearchAssistant

13. _____ is defined by the American _____ Association as the activity, set of institutions, and processes for creating, communicating, delivering, and exchanging offerings that have value for customers, clients, partners, and society at large. The term developed from the original meaning which referred literally to going to market, as in shopping, or going to a market to sell goods or services.

_____ practice tends to be seen as a creative industry, which includes advertising, distribution and selling.

a. Customer acquisition management
b. Marketing
c. Product naming
d. Marketing myopia

14. A _____ is a written document that details the necessary actions to achieve one or more marketing objectives. It can be for a product or service, a brand, or a product line. _____s cover between one and five years.

a. Disruptive technology
b. Marketing strategy
c. Prosumer
d. Marketing plan

15. _____ is a marketing term, and involves evaluating the situation and trends in a particular company's market. _____ is often called the 'three c's', which refers to the three major elements that must be studied:

- Customers
- Costs
- Competition

Chapter 12. Organizing and Planning for Effective Implementation

The number of 'c's' is sometimes extended to four, five, or even six, with 'Collaboration', 'Company', and 'Competitive advantage'.

- Marketing mix
- SWOT analysis

a. Power III
b. 180SearchAssistant
c. 6-3-5 Brainwriting
d. Situation analysis

Chapter 13. Measuring and Delivering Marketing Performance

1. _____ is defined by the American _____ Association as the activity, set of institutions, and processes for creating, communicating, delivering, and exchanging offerings that have value for customers, clients, partners, and society at large. The term developed from the original meaning which referred literally to going to market, as in shopping, or going to a market to sell goods or services.

   _____ practice tends to be seen as a creative industry, which includes advertising, distribution and selling.

   a. Customer acquisition management
   b. Product naming
   c. Marketing
   d. Marketing myopia

2. The general definition of an _____ is an evaluation of a person, organization, system, process, project or product. _____s are performed to ascertain the validity and reliability of information; also to provide an assessment of a system's internal control. The goal of an _____ is to express an opinion on the person/organization/system (etc) in question, under evaluation based on work done on a test basis.
   a. AMAX
   b. ADTECH
   c. ACNielsen
   d. Audit

3. _____ is the process whereby an organization establishes the parameters within which programs, investments, and acquisitions are reaching the desired results. Performance Reference Model of the Federal Enterprise Architecture, 2005.

   This process of measuring performance often requires the use of statistical evidence to determine progress toward specific defined organizational objectives.

   There are many types of measurements.

   a. Voice of the customer
   b. Crisis management
   c. Digital strategy
   d. Performance measurement

4. In economics, business, retail, and accounting, a _____ is the value of money that has been used up to produce something, and hence is not available for use anymore. In economics, a _____ is an alternative that is given up as a result of a decision. In business, the _____ may be one of acquisition, in which case the amount of money expended to acquire it is counted as _____.

Chapter 13. Measuring and Delivering Marketing Performance

a. Fixed costs
b. Variable cost
c. Transaction cost
d. Cost

5. _____ is a costing model that identifies activities in an organization and assigns the cost of each activity resource to all products and services according to the actual consumption by each: it assigns more indirect costs (overhead) into direct costs.

In this way an organization can establish the true cost of its individual products and services for the purposes of identifying and eliminating those which are unprofitable and lowering the prices of those which are overpriced.

In a business organization, the ABC methodology assigns an organization's resource costs through activities to the products and services provided to its customers.

a. ACNielsen
b. AMAX
c. ADTECH
d. Activity-based costing

6. _____, a business term, is a measure of how products and services supplied by a company meet or surpass customer expectation. It is seen as a key performance indicator within business and is part of the four perspectives of a Balanced Scorecard.

In a competitive marketplace where businesses compete for customers, _____ is seen as a key differentiator and increasingly has become a key element of business strategy.

a. Supplier diversity
b. Psychological pricing
c. Customer base
d. Customer satisfaction

7. _____ describes the situation when output from (or information about the result of) an event or phenomenon in the past will influence the same event/phenomenon in the present or future. When an event is part of a chain of cause-and-effect that forms a circuit or loop, then the event is said to 'feed back' into itself.

Chapter 13. Measuring and Delivering Marketing Performance

_____ is also a synonym for:

- _____ Signal; the information about the initial event that is the basis for subsequent modification of the event.
- _____ Loop; the causal path that leads from the initial generation of the _____ signal to the subsequent modification of the event.

_____ is a mechanism, process or signal that is looped back to control a system within itself. Such a loop is called a _____ loop.

a. 180SearchAssistant
b. 6-3-5 Brainwriting
c. Power III
d. Feedback

8. _____ refer to a collection of facts usually collected as the result of experience, observation or experiment or a set of premises. This may consist of numbers, words particularly as measurements or observations of a set of variables. _____ are often viewed as a lowest level of abstraction from which information and knowledge are derived.

a. Mean
b. Pearson product-moment correlation coefficient
c. Sample size
d. Data

9. 'Speaking generally, properties are those physical quantities which directly describe the physical attributes of the system; _____s are those combinations of the properties which suffice to determine the response of the system. Properties can have all sorts of dimensions, depending upon the system being considered; _____s are dimensionless, or have the dimension of time or its reciprocal.'

The term can also be used in engineering contexts, however, as it is typically used in the physical sciences.

When the terms formal _____ and actual _____ are used, they generally correspond with the definitions used in computer science.

a. 6-3-5 Brainwriting
b. Parameter
c. Power III
d. 180SearchAssistant

Chapter 13. Measuring and Delivering Marketing Performance

10. Procter is a surname, and may also refer to:

    - Bryan Waller Procter (pseud. Barry Cornwall), English poet
    - Goodwin Procter, American law firm
    - _____, consumer products multinational

    a. Black PRies
    b. Procter ' Gamble
    c. Convergent
    d. Flyer

11. In accounting, _____ has a very specific meaning. It is an outflow of cash or other valuable assets from a person or company to another person or company. This outflow of cash is generally one side of a trade for products or services that have equal or better current or future value to the buyer than to the seller.

    a. ACNielsen
    b. Expense
    c. ADTECH
    d. AMAX

12. The _____ is a marketing term and refers to all of the forces outside of marketing that affect marketing management's ability to build and maintain successful relationships with target customers. The _____ consists of both the macroenvironment and the microenvironment.

    The microenvironment refers to the forces that are close to the company and affect its ability to serve its customers.

    a. Customer franchise
    b. Psychographic
    c. Business-to-consumer
    d. Market environment

13. _____ is understood as a business unit within the overall corporate identity which is distinguishable from other business because it serves a defined external market where management can conduct strategic planning in relation to products and markets. When companies become really large, they are best thought of as being composed of a number of businesses (or _____s.)

    In the broader domain of strategic management, the phrase '_____' came into use in the 1960s, largely as a result of General Electric's many units.

Chapter 13. Measuring and Delivering Marketing Performance

a. Corporate strategy
b. Cost leadership
c. Business strategy
d. Strategic business unit

14. Human beings are also considered to be _____ because they have the ability to change raw materials into valuable _____. The term Human _____ can also be defined as the skills, energies, talents, abilities and knowledge that are used for the production of goods or the rendering of services. While taking into account human beings as _____, the following things have to be kept in mind:

- The size of the population
- The capabilities of the individuals in that population

Many _____ cannot be consumed in their original form. They have to be processed in order to change them into more usable commodities.

a. 180SearchAssistant
b. Resources
c. 6-3-5 Brainwriting
d. Power III

15. _____ is a form of communication that typically attempts to persuade potential customers to purchase or to consume more of a particular brand of product or service. 'While now central to the contemporary global economy and the reproduction of global production networks, it is only quite recently that _____ has been more than a marginal influence on patterns of sales and production. The formation of modern _____ was intimately bound up with the emergence of new forms of monopoly capitalism around the end of the 19th and beginning of the 20th century as one element in corporate strategies to create, organize and where possible control markets, especially for mass produced consumer goods.

a. ACNielsen
b. Advertising
c. AMAX
d. ADTECH

16. _____ is one of the four elements of marketing mix. An organization or set of organizations (go-betweens) involved in the process of making a product or service available for use or consumption by a consumer or business user.

The other three parts of the marketing mix are product, pricing, and promotion.

Chapter 13. Measuring and Delivering Marketing Performance

a. Comparison-Shopping agent
b. Japan Advertising Photographers' Association
c. Distribution
d. Better Living Through Chemistry

17. _____ in organizations and public policy is both the organizational process of creating and maintaining a plan; and the psychological process of thinking about the activities required to create a desired goal on some scale. As such, it is a fundamental property of intelligent behavior. This thought process is essential to the creation and refinement of a plan, or integration of it with other plans, that is, it combines forecasting of developments with the preparation of scenarios of how to react to them.

a. 6-3-5 Brainwriting
b. Power III
c. Planning
d. 180SearchAssistant

18. _____ in economics and business is the result of an exchange and from that trade we assign a numerical monetary value to a good, service or asset. If I trade 4 apples for an orange, the _____ of an orange is 4 - apples. Inversely, the _____ of an apple is 1/4 oranges.

a. Discounts and allowances
b. Price
c. Contribution margin-based pricing
d. Pricing

19. A _____ researches, selects, develops, and places a company's products.

A _____ considers numerous factors such as target demographic, the products offered by the competition, and how well the product fits in with the company's business model. Generally, a _____ manages one or more tangible products.

a. Promotional mix
b. Power III
c. Pick and pack
d. Product manager

20. A _____ is a list of the general tasks and responsibilities of a position. Typically, it also includes to whom the position reports, specifications such as the qualifications needed by the person in the job, salary range for the position, etc. A _____ is usually developed by conducting a job analysis, which includes examining the tasks and sequences of tasks necessary to perform the job.

Chapter 13. Measuring and Delivering Marketing Performance

a. Job description
b. 6-3-5 Brainwriting
c. 180SearchAssistant
d. Power III

21. _____ in economics refers to metrics and measures of output from production processes, per unit of input. Labor _____, for example, is typically measured as a ratio of output per labor-hour, an input. _____ may be conceived of as a metrics of the technical or engineering efficiency of production.

a. Productivity
b. Value engineering
c. 180SearchAssistant
d. Power III

22. A _____ is a plan of action designed to achieve a particular goal.

_____ is different from tactics. In military terms, tactics is concerned with the conduct of an engagement while _____ is concerned with how different engagements are linked.

a. 6-3-5 Brainwriting
b. 180SearchAssistant
c. Strategy
d. Power III

ANSWER KEY

Chapter 1
1. a   2. a   3. b   4. c   5. c   6. d   7. b   8. d   9. c   10. d
11. c   12. c   13. c   14. b   15. d   16. d   17. d   18. d   19. c   20. d

Chapter 2
1. d   2. a   3. a   4. a   5. b   6. d   7. d   8. d   9. d   10. b
11. b   12. d   13. c   14. d   15. d   16. d   17. a   18. d   19. d   20. d
21. d   22. b   23. a   24. d   25. d

Chapter 3
1. d   2. d   3. c   4. d   5. d   6. d   7. a   8. c   9. c   10. d
11. d   12. d   13. d   14. d   15. a   16. c   17. d

Chapter 4
1. b   2. d   3. d   4. d   5. d   6. a   7. d   8. d   9. a   10. c
11. a   12. b   13. d   14. c   15. a   16. c   17. b   18. d   19. d

Chapter 5
1. a   2. d   3. d   4. d   5. d   6. b   7. d   8. d   9. d   10. d
11. d   12. d   13. c   14. d   15. c   16. a   17. b   18. a   19. a   20. a
21. c   22. a   23. d   24. b

Chapter 6
1. d   2. b   3. b   4. a   5. c   6. c   7. b   8. d   9. d   10. d
11. d

Chapter 7
1. d   2. d   3. d   4. c   5. d   6. a   7. a   8. d   9. c   10. d
11. a   12. d   13. a

Chapter 8
1. d   2. b   3. d   4. d   5. d   6. b   7. d   8. b   9. d   10. d
11. a   12. b   13. c   14. b   15. d   16. c   17. a   18. d   19. b   20. d
21. d   22. b   23. d   24. d   25. b   26. d   27. a   28. d   29. b

Chapter 9
1. c   2. b   3. d

Chapter 10
1. d   2. a   3. c   4. b   5. c   6. d   7. d   8. c   9. b   10. a
11. d   12. d   13. d   14. d   15. d   16. d

ANSWER KEY

Chapter 11
1. b	2. c	3. d	4. a	5. d	6. d	7. d	8. c	9. d	10. d
11. b	12. d	13. d	14. d	15. a	16. d	17. b	18. d	19. b	20. d
21. b	22. d	23. a	24. d	25. d	26. c	27. b	28. d	29. d	30. b
31. d	32. a	33. d							

Chapter 12
1. a	2. d	3. c	4. b	5. d	6. d	7. d	8. b	9. b	10. d
11. a	12. c	13. b	14. d	15. d					

Chapter 13
1. c	2. d	3. d	4. d	5. d	6. d	7. d	8. d	9. b	10. b
11. b	12. d	13. d	14. b	15. b	16. c	17. c	18. b	19. d	20. a
21. a	22. c								

www.ingramcontent.com/pod-product-compliance
Lightning Source LLC
Chambersburg PA
CBHW081848230426

43669CB00018B/2871